DOLLHOUSE

DOLLHOUSE

⊰ A PLAY ⊱

REBECCA GILMAN

Based on *A Doll's House* by Henrik Ibsen

NORTHWESTERN UNIVERSITY PRESS

EVANSTON, ILLINOIS

Northwestern University Press
www.nupress.northwestern.edu

Printed in the United States of America

10   9   8   7   6   5   4   3   2

LIBRARY OF CONGRESS
CATALOGING-IN-PUBLICATION DATA

Gilman, Rebecca Claire.
    Dollhouse : a play / Rebecca Gilman.
        p. cm.
    "Based on A Doll's House by Henrik Ibsen."
    ISBN 978-0-8101-2631-2 (pbk. : alk. paper) 1. Married people—Illinois—Chicago—Drama. 2. Lincoln Park (Chicago, Ill.)—Drama. I. Ibsen, Henrik, 1828–1906. Dukkehjem. II. Title.
    PS3557.I456D65 2010
    812.54—dc22
                                2009044646

∞ The paper used in this publication meets the minimum requirements of the American National Standard for Information Sciences—Permanence of Paper for Printed Library Materials, ANSI Z39.48-1992.

All photographs copyright © Michael Brosilow; taken at the Goodman Theatre production.

CONTENTS

PRODUCTION HISTORY

Dollhouse premiered at the Goodman Theatre in Chicago on June 19, 2005. It was directed by Robert Falls. Sets were designed by Robert Brill, costumes by Mara Blumenfeld, lighting by James F. Ingalls, and sound by Richard Woodbury. Choreography was by Randy Duncan. Video projections were compiled by Rene Arteaga. The dramaturge was Tom Creamer, and the stage manager was Alden Vasquez. The cast was as follows:

Nora Helmer . . . . Maggie Siff
Iris . . . . Maritza Cervantes
Terry Helmer . . . . Anthony Starke
Pete . . . . Lance Stuart Baker
Kristine Linde . . . . Elizabeth Rich
Marta . . . . Charin Alvarez
Max . . . . Ryan Cowhey, Matthew Gerdisch
Macey . . . . Jordyn Knysz, Emily Leahy
Skyler . . . . Melody Hollis, Allison Sparrow
Raj Patel . . . . Firdous Bamji

A very special thanks to Robert Falls for the inspiration and guidance that made this play possible. Thank you, too, to Kat Falls, John McKinnon, and Jim Annable for the plot points and economic advice. And, as always, love and thank you to Charles for everything.

DOLLHOUSE

CHARACTERS

Nora Helmer, thirty-two

Iris, thirty

Terry Helmer, thirty-three

Pete, thirty-three

Kristine Linde, thirty-four

Marta, thirty

Max, four

Macey, three

Skyler, six

Raj Patel, thirty-three

Time: December 2004.

Place: A condo in west Lincoln Park, Chicago.

ACT 1

[*At rise, the family room and kitchen of a new-construction three-flat in the Lincoln Park neighborhood of Chicago. It has an open floor plan, with a kitchen opening onto a living room and dining area. It is very fashionably and tastefully decorated. A leather sofa and chair sit before a working fireplace. There are built-in bookcases, some books, lots of framed wedding photos, and photos of children. The room has indirect lighting. A lot of thought has gone into everything in the room, but nothing is hyperexpensive. It's all Pottery Barn or Crate and Barrel– level stuff. The kitchen has granite countertops, cherry cabinets, stainless steel appliances, and a Viking refrigerator—all the extras the developer offered. Prominent on one wall is a professional black-and-white photograph. It's a large portrait—say, three by five feet—of a very pregnant* NORA. TERRY *stands behind her, with his arms around her stomach. He is gazing at her.* NORA *is gazing at the camera, looking fully satisfied and happy. A decorated Christmas tree stands in a corner, with lots of presents underneath it. On the dining-room table stands a Christmas centerpiece; decorations line the mantel. In a corner is a Rubbermaid container full of children's toys. The front door is off- stage, down a short entryway with a hallstand or hooks for coats. Other doors lead to* TERRY's *study and to the TV room and bedrooms. There is a back entrance as well. The door to* TERRY's *study is closed.* NORA *enters through the entryway, loaded down with shopping bags. She is followed by* IRIS, *the cleaning woman, with more bags. A couple of the bags are from Target. It is the Saturday before Christmas.*]

NORA: Is Terry home?

IRIS: He's in his office. You want me to get him?

NORA: No. [*Sorting through the bags, pulling some items out for* IRIS *to hide*] Iris, here, let's take these . . . and these and put them in the hall closet.

IRIS: You got a lot of stuff.

NORA: And here . . .

[NORA *reaches into a Target bag and pulls out a gift card.*]

I'm sorry I didn't have a chance to wrap it. [*As* IRIS *opens it*] It's just a gift card. But I didn't want to buy you something you don't need . . .

IRIS: Sure, sure.

NORA: It's for two hundred dollars.

IRIS: Two hundred dollars? Thanks!

NORA: You're welcome. Merry Christmas.

IRIS: Thanks a lot.

NORA: Now let's put these up so nobody's surprise is ruined.

IRIS [*picking up the bags*]: You're really nice.

NORA [*laughing*]: I'm glad you think so.

IRIS [*heading for the hall*]: You really like to shop.

NORA: I had a huge list.

[IRIS *exits.* NORA *reaches into a bag and pulls out a small, Chinese-style takeout box tied with a burgundy ribbon. She opens it and pulls out a truffle and puts the whole thing into her mouth.*]

TERRY [*off, from his study*]: No-No? You home?

NORA [*trying to chew*]: Hmmm?

[NORA *shoves the box and ribbon into her purse.*]

TERRY [*off*]: Where you been?

NORA: Nowhere.

[NORA *tries to swallow the truffle with her back to his study door.*]

TERRY [*off*]: What are you up to?

NORA [*wiping her mouth*]: Nothing.

TERRY [*off*]: What kind of nothing?

[*Small beat.*]

Nora?

[TERRY *opens the study door.*]

Did you go shopping again?

NORA: I had a huge list.

TERRY: What's the damage?

NORA: Everything was on sale.

TERRY [*looking into the bags*]: Nothing's on sale at Christmas.

NORA: I went to Target.

TERRY: Oh God . . .

NORA: I had to get all these little things for people. And I got Iris a gift card.

TERRY: Who's Iris?

NORA: The cleaning woman, Terry. She's right down the hall.

TERRY: We got a new one?

NORA: Three months ago.

TERRY: How much?

NORA: You write the checks—

TERRY: No, how much was the gift card?

NORA: Fifty.

[*Small beat.*]

What? Was that too much?

TERRY [*looking down the hall*]: I don't even know who she is . . .

NORA: I got her some soap too.

TERRY: Is she dirty?

NORA: I got everybody soap. I read about it in *Real Simple*. [*Opening the Target bag*] They're these nice soaps, but they're really cheap—

TERRY: How cheap?

NORA: Three dollars. [*Pulling two bars of soap out*] See? Lavender and verbena—

[TERRY *smells a bar of soap.*]

TERRY: Don't most people buy their own soap?

NORA: It's fancy soap.

TERRY: It better be fancy.

NORA: You have no idea how much the real stuff costs.

[NORA *pours a couple of dozen bars of soap out of the bag.*]

I'm going to put them in little stacks and tie ribbons around them.

TERRY: For who?

NORA: Iris. And Lindley, at Gymboree . . .

TERRY: You mean that person who gets paid for her services?

NORA: She probably makes, like, six bucks an hour. And she's so good with the kids. So I got her some soap. Okay?

[*Beat.*]

Are you mad?

TERRY: It's just . . . you've been buying a lot of Christmas presents . . .

NORA: This is it.

TERRY: I thought this was it last week.

NORA: I'm at the Gymboree girl. I'm through.

TERRY: Which card did you use?

NORA: Fleet.

TERRY: So are we maxed out on that one now?

NORA: No.

TERRY: I really want to pay off our credit cards.

NORA: We will. When you get your bonus.

TERRY: That's not a sure thing.

NORA: It's part of your promotion.

TERRY: I have to meet plan—

NORA: Why wouldn't you meet plan?

TERRY: I don't know. I could get hit by a truck tomorrow. Somebody could blow up the building—

NORA: Don't talk like that. I can't think things like that.

TERRY: My point is, I don't have the bonus. I don't even have the raise yet, and we'll never pay off the credit cards if you keep charging things on the credit cards. It's simple math.

[*Beat.*]

NORA: I'll take it all back.

TERRY: I'm not saying take it back—

NORA [*overlapping*]: It's not important. I'll take it back.

TERRY: I'm not saying take it back, I'm just saying—

[*Small beat.*]

Promise me this is it.

NORA: I promise. I promise I promise I promise.

[NORA *smiles.* TERRY *relents.*]

Did you invite Dr. Pete to dinner?

TERRY: Yeah. Maybe— Should I get some champagne?

NORA: Why not?

TERRY: I got a promotion. And a bonus. We can celebrate.

NORA: I was thinking after the New Year maybe we could start looking at houses . . .

TERRY [*angrily*]: We're getting out of debt first, okay?!

[*Beat.*]

I thought you understood that. We can't go buy a new house *and* send the kids to private school *and* buy everybody on the planet *soap.*

[*Small beat.*]

[*Tiredly*] Nora, I only want a few months . . . just a few months where I'm not scrambling. A few months where maybe you don't ask for something huge?

[*Pause.*]

NORA: Of course. I'm sorry.

TERRY: You're just like your father.

NORA: No I'm not.

TERRY: He made money disappear.

NORA: He wanted us to be happy.

[NORA *regards him.*]

Don't be mad. I'll sing you a song.

TERRY: Don't sing me a song.

NORA: Oh yes. You want a song. I can tell.

[NORA *picks up a bar of soap.*]

To the theme of *All Things Considered.* [*Doing a little dance with the soap*] Fan-cy fan-cy fan-cy fan-cy, fan-cy fan-cy fan-cy SOAP! Deetle deet, deetely deetely deetle deet.

[TERRY *smiles. He holds up the Target bag.*]

I wasn't all bad. I got all this on sale. Saline solution. Toothpaste . . .

TERRY: You take good care of us, Mommy.

[*He gives her a kiss.*]

NORA: And you're my little boy.

[*She rubs his head.*]

TERRY: It's getting thinner, isn't it?

NORA: No.

TERRY [*pointing to his hairline*]: It looked thin to me this morning. Through here.

NORA: You're obsessing.

TERRY: Bald men are pathetic.

NORA: Bald men are sexy.

TERRY: Only if they're rich.

NORA: Then you have nothing to worry about. The future is bright.

TERRY: That's not our future. That's the light, reflecting off my bald head.

[*He looks at the packages.*]

You're right. The kids should have a good year. [*Indicating the bags*] What'd you get them?

NORA: Do you want to do the receipts?

TERRY: May as well.

[*She reaches into her purse, pulls out an envelope, and gives him the receipts inside. He looks at the first one.*]

Red Balloon?

[*She picks up a bag.*]

NORA: I got three things at Red Balloon. I got Skyler a sweater.

[*She pulls it out.*]

Fifty dollars, but it was on sale.

[*She pulls out a pair of baby socks.*]

And I got Macey these little socks. See? They have little high heels on them.

[*She pulls out a knitted stuffed monkey.*]

And I got Max a monkey.

TERRY [*looking at the receipts*]: Did you get yourself anything?

NORA: I don't want anything.

TERRY: Then what am I going to get you for Christmas?

NORA: Nothing.

TERRY: You have to want something.

[*Small beat.*]

NORA: Cash?

TERRY [*laughing*]: Cash?

NORA: Some cash would be nice.

TERRY: But I want to get you something nice.

NORA: You could tie a little ribbon around it.

TERRY: What are you going to do with cash?

NORA: Spend it. On something stupid. I don't know.

[*Small beat.*]

I always feel self-conscious about the things I buy because I know . . . we go over the receipts. Except for groceries or whatever, I never have, like, cash. Like, mad money. Like when we got all those checks for our wedding.

TERRY: So I should just give you . . . what? Twenty bucks?

NORA: Whatever you want would be fine.

[TERRY *takes out his wallet.*]

TERRY: Okay.

[*He hands her a twenty.*]

    Merry Christmas.

[NORA *looks at it.*]

NORA: Thanks.

TERRY: Oh for God's sake.

[*He pulls out all the bills and gives them to her.*]

    Here.

NORA: Thank you!

TERRY: That's really what you want?

NORA: Yes. [*Counting it*] Thank you thank you thank you!

TERRY: Make sure you really buy yourself something, okay?

NORA: Yay! Money!

[*She kisses him.* TERRY *stops kissing her.*]

TERRY: What are you up to, anyway?

NORA: What do you mean?

[TERRY *studies her.*]

TERRY: You didn't happen to stumble into that chocolate place, did you?

NORA: No.

TERRY: You didn't buy yourself a little treat?

NORA: I told you I wouldn't.

TERRY: Not even one little truffle?

NORA: No!

TERRY: All right.

[*A knocking can be heard at the back door as it opens.* PETE *enters. He is very at home here.*]

PETE: Happy Horror Days.

TERRY: Dr. Pete.

NORA: You're early.

[PETE *puts his coat on a chair. He takes a leather CD case out of his coat pocket.*]

PETE: We're going to burn a CD. [*Looking at all the packages*] Where's my present?

[TERRY *picks up a bar of soap, hands it to him.*]

TERRY: Here.

PETE: Thanks.

NORA [*taking the soap*]: Stop it! He's making fun of my soap.

TERRY [*apologizing*]: I'm not making fun of your soap. It's nice soap.

NORA: Yeah yeah . . .

[NORA *smiles at* TERRY. *He smiles back.*]

TERRY: She always gets me with that face.

PETE: Yep.

TERRY [*to* PETE]: Let's go in my office.

NORA: Who's the CD for?

PETE: My nephew. He's into all this techno dance bullshit. I'm gonna teach him what real rock and roll is.

TERRY: The Eagles.

PETE [*to* NORA]: Your husband's a dork.

[TERRY *and* PETE *exit.* NORA *takes out the money* TERRY *gave her and sits down. She counts the bills, rearranging them so they all face the same way.*]

NORA [*under her breath*]: Twenty, forty, sixty . . .

[*The doorbell rings.*]

　　Oh—Kristine— [*Yelling*] Iris?

IRIS [*off*]: I got it!

NORA [*calling to* IRIS]: That's my friend Kristine. Tell her to come on back.

[NORA *puts the money into her purse and starts to straighten up.* KRISTINE *enters, dressed for winter and carrying a gift bag.*]

KRISTINE: Hi Nora.

NORA: Kristine?

KRISTINE: Am I early?

NORA: No, I— No, no. Look at you.

KRISTINE: Do we have to?

NORA: You look great.

KRISTINE: No I don't.

NORA: You do. You look great.

KRISTINE: I look old.

NORA: No. You look different, is all. If you look old it's just because . . . well it's been ten years.

KRISTINE: I know—

NORA: Oh my God, Kristine!

[NORA *gives* KRISTINE *a big hug.*]

KRISTINE [*laughing*]: Nora.

NORA: Don't look at this mess.

KRISTINE: I love your place.

NORA: Thanks.

[KRISTINE *sees the portrait.*]

KRISTINE: Is that Terry?

NORA: That's when I was pregnant with Max.

KRISTINE: He's the oldest?

NORA: Middle.

KRISTINE: It's great.

[*She hands* NORA *the bag and takes off her coat.*]

I brought you a little present.

NORA: That's so sweet.

[*She pulls a box of tea bags out of the bag.*]

KRISTINE: They're little individual tea bags.

NORA [*overlapping*]: Stand-alone tea bags. I love these. Thank you. Can I make you some?

KRISTINE: I'd love some. I'm not used to this cold. I have to get reacclimated.

NORA: You need some good boots.

[NORA *hangs up* KRISTINE's *coat, and then starts making tea. They drink the tea during the following scene.*]

KRISTINE [*looking at* NORA's *shopping bags*]: Have you done all your shopping?

NORA: I'm finally through. I kind of went overboard, but—well—Terry got a promotion . . .

KRISTINE: Really?

NORA: Division Head Manager. At Bank One.

KRISTINE: That's terrific. What department?

NORA: Mid-Market Lending.

KRISTINE: Good for him.

NORA: Yeah, so—

[*She smiles.*]

You know. Bonus and everything. So I'm celebrating. My dad always said, "Use it while you got it."

[*She laughs.*]

You know, there's a reason rich people are so happy.

KRISTINE: You have a safety net.

NORA: It's more than a safety net. It's a big pile of cash.

KRISTINE: Well. Congratulations.

NORA: So you moved back from Atlanta?

KRISTINE [*nods*]: I was with Arthur Andersen.

NORA: Oh.

KRISTINE: We didn't have anything to do with Enron. But . . . one bad apple as they say.

NORA: They'll bounce back, though.

KRISTINE: I doubt it.

NORA: But these things go in cycles.

[*Small beat.*]

KRISTINE: So you guys have kids?

NORA: Three. Skyler's six, Max is four, and Macey just turned three. And you?

KRISTINE: Still single. No kids.

NORA: Have you not met the right person, or . . . ?

KRISTINE: I don't know. Too much work.

NORA: You always worked so hard. We'd be like, "Thursday night drink specials!" and you'd be, "Tax exam tomorrow."

KRISTINE: I took the whole R.A. thing too seriously.

NORA: Have you found a place?

KRISTINE: I signed a lease on a one-bedroom.

NORA: An apartment?

KRISTINE: Yes.

NORA: You should buy something. Our friends are all buying single-families closer to the lake; they're all in venture capital or they cashed in on some dot-com—

KRISTINE: I heard Raj Patel's made a fortune. In a biotech start-up.

NORA: Yeah.

[*Small beat.*]

But anyway, that's what I want to do. Buy a house. I want something further east. Ideally Gold Coast but everything in our price range there is in a high-rise. And I'd want something vintage anyway. Something with some history. There are still farmhouses around here.

KRISTINE: I didn't know that.

NORA: This was all pasture back in the day. That's why you can still find places with double lots. That's what I want. A real yard, you know, so the kids can have a swing set. And I can plant perennials. I love that word. When I was a kid, we moved all the time. Daddy only saw real estate as an investment, so I never had a sense of home.

KRISTINE: I lived in the same house for eighteen years and I never had a sense of home.

NORA: Family's so important, for that.

KRISTINE: When would you move?

NORA: Oh I don't know. I wish we had started further east, but when we first started looking, we were having a hard time. My dad was sick and Terry was . . . had to take a leave of absence . . .

[*She stops.*]

So we're lucky we didn't end up in Albany Park.

KRISTINE: Where's that?

NORA: Exactly! Where is that.

KRISTINE: No. Seriously. Where is it?

NORA: All the way at the end of the Brown Line.

[*Beat.*]

KRISTINE: Well I'm glad everything worked out.

NORA: It almost didn't. Except, well it's a whole story—

KRISTINE: I don't need to know, if it's personal.

[NORA *looks at* KRISTINE, *deciding.*]

NORA: No, it's okay. I want to tell you. I always used to tell you everything, didn't I?

KRISTINE: I was an R.A. Everybody told me everything.

NORA: We had some bad luck, is all. It was six years ago. I was pregnant with Skyler. Terry was playing basketball with some of his buddies and he slipped and completely destroyed his knee—

KRISTINE: God.

NORA: It was a freak thing. They had to do surgery to repair the tendon but it never healed right and it kept hurting him. They sent him to rehab but it was a joke. He'd stand on one leg and throw a ball at a trampoline. So we finally went back to the orthopedic guy and his solution was to hand Terry a prescription for Vicodin.

KRISTINE: Isn't that addictive?

NORA: It's a narcotic. It's highly addictive. But nobody told us that. And it decreases in efficacy, the longer you take it. So you end up taking more and more.

[*Small beat.*]

And he got addicted. Basically. It's a highly addictive drug.

KRISTINE: Did you know?

NORA: I didn't want to know. We'd put an offer down on the condo and I had this picture, you know, our first home, our family together. It's new construction and I wanted to pick out the colors and fixtures. So I never asked Terry what was wrong. Because I didn't want anything to be wrong.

KRISTINE: It's easy to be in denial.

NORA: I'm afraid it's a trait I inherited from my dad. He wasn't exactly a "reality-based" kind of guy. If he was broke, to cheer himself up, he'd go buy a horse.

KRISTINE: Didn't your dad own a lamp factory?

NORA: Lighting fixtures and lamps. It went out of business.

[*Beat.*]

KRISTINE: So did Terry finally tell you? About the pills?

NORA: He was missing work, going around to doctors for prescriptions. Then he started getting sick, vomiting and dizzy and passing out, then one day, it was awful, he was changing Skyler and he dropped her.

KRISTINE: Jesus.

NORA: She was okay, thank God. But I knew then.

[*Small beat.*]

I think . . . he was so ashamed. It killed him that he had let this stupid drug get the better of him.

KRISTINE: It wasn't his fault.

NORA: That's what I said. Immediately. It's an illness. But he was so embarrassed, he didn't want anybody to find out. So I found this place called Sierra Tucson, in Arizona? They have this outstanding rehab program. It's thirty thousand dollars—but Terry worked so hard and we did all the counseling and everything and he's been clean ever since.

KRISTINE: I'm so glad.

NORA: Please don't tell him I told you.

KRISTINE: I won't.

NORA: Nobody knows except for Dr. Pete, and now you.

KRISTINE: I won't tell anybody.

NORA: I know you won't. You're so good. In college you were so smart. You were the only smart friend I had. I always felt like there must be something decent in me if you liked me.

KRISTINE: I thought you were a riot.

NORA: Nobody at the bank knows. That's why Terry took the leave of absence. He told everyone we had to take care of my father. It actually worked out, in a weird way, my dad's being sick? It explained everything and then when Daddy died he left us some money, so we were able to cover everything. The rehab, the condo . . .

KRISTINE: I'm so sorry, Nora.

NORA: We put on a good face. But it completely sucked. Everything about it completely sucked.

KRISTINE: You had Skyler.

NORA: I had Skyler! That didn't suck. You're right.

[*She looks at the portrait on the wall.*]

Although I wish we could have gotten a picture with her. Most people do their first, but we couldn't afford it. [*Turning back to* KRISTINE] I have to think if I know any single guys for you.

KRISTINE: That's okay.

NORA: We have to get you married.

KRISTINE: I don't want to get married.

NORA: But you want to have kids.

KRISTINE [*bemused*]: No.

NORA: Wow. See? You were always like that.

[*Small beat.*]

KRISTINE: Where are the kids?

NORA: Marta took them ice skating.

KRISTINE: And Marta is . . .

NORA: Our nanny.

KRISTINE: So you're working?

NORA: I used to work. At a gallery, in the Merchandise Mart? Or, not a real gallery. We sold very big canvases to very big corporations. More interior decorating really. Which is . . . it's goofy but I like that. I remember once, my mom took me to the Art Institute when I was little, and the thing I loved most were the miniature rooms. The little drawing rooms with the settees and the harpsichords and the little vases of tulips. There's one that even has a little cat curled up in front of the fireplace. They're so perfect. Because they don't have any people.

KRISTINE [*overlapping*]: There are no people.

[*They laugh.*]

NORA: My poor mom was like, "Look at the Picasso." I was like, "Look at the tiny candlesticks."

KRISTINE: So why did you quit?

NORA: It didn't even pay enough to cover child care.

KRISTINE: Maybe you can go back to it. When the kids are older.

NORA: I don't know. I don't really want to be an interior decorator, I just, I want to do something creative. I bought that book, *The Artist's Way*? Do you know that book?

KRISTINE: No.

[NORA *gets it off a bookshelf and hands it to* KRISTINE.]

NORA: It's kind of dumb, I guess, but it helps you figure out how to get in touch with your creative side, you know? To express yourself. It has these exercises where you picture things you want, dreams and goals and settings too. There's an exercise where you go through magazines and pull out pictures of places and things that inspire you. So I did all the exercises, and at the end I realized, I don't want to paint or write or anything. I'm not talented like that. But I am creative, in that I think I can create a world where beautiful things can exist. Like a Virginia Woolf sort of thing where the food is right, the wine is right, then you find the perfect centerpiece and that brings the table together, and that brings the people together and you have a perfect dinner party. Or, like, if I were really rich I'd be Peggy Guggenheim. I'd have my Jackson Pollock in the hallway, and my Noguchi in the living room. And I'd, like, preside. Over my domain.

[NORA *laughs.*]

It's silly, I know . . .

KRISTINE [*handing the book back to* NORA]: No. It's nice you have time to do this sort of thing.

NORA [*taking the book, hurt*]: You're so sweet. I showed it to Dr. Pete and he said it was stay-at-home-mom bullshit.

KRISTINE: Now who's Dr. Pete?

NORA: Pete. He's Terry's old roommate. He's an endocrinologist. You'd like him. He's got a really dry sense of humor and a great practice—

KRISTINE: I'm really not looking to date anybody.

NORA: Well, you would love him, but he's . . . he's our closest friend.

[NORA *smiles at* KRISTINE, *happy to see her.*]

God. I've been babbling. I haven't even asked you why you moved to Chicago.

KRISTINE: For the most boring reason of all: I need a job.

NORA: Because of Arthur Andersen?

KRISTINE: I had some money saved up—I actually took some time off, after everything collapsed—and traveled. It was kind of nice. But now I think I made a mistake, because the job market's terrible and I really need to find something.

NORA: And you just moved. That's so stressful. You know, if you want to relax someplace, there are some really cute spas in Saugatuck—

KRISTINE: I can't go to a spa, Nora. I don't have a job.

NORA: I just meant . . . you look tired.

KRISTINE: I know.

[*Beat.*]

I'm sorry. It's not your fault.

NORA: It's Enron's fault.

[KRISTINE *smiles.*]

You know, Terry's looking to hire some people.

KRISTINE: Well, I did think—when you said he got the promotion—

NORA: Oh! Leave it to me. I'll use my feminine wiles.

[*Small beat.*]

KRISTINE: Maybe I should talk to him.

NORA: I can talk to him.

KRISTINE: You don't even know what sort of work I did.

NORA: What'd you do?

KRISTINE: Transaction services.

[*Small beat.*]

It's okay if you don't know what it is—

NORA: I know what it is. Just because I was an art history major doesn't mean I don't understand business. I understand business.

KRISTINE: Sure you do—

NORA: I'm tired of people treating me like I don't know anything.

KRISTINE: That's not what I meant.

[*Pause.*]

NORA: Do you think this is normal? Terry won't let me have an ATM card.

KRISTINE: What—? What do you do for money?

NORA: He gives me an allowance, for household expenses, and anything extra I have to put on the credit card. But then he makes me keep every receipt and at the end of the month he sits down and compares it to the statement, item by item. Then I justify everything I bought.

[*Beat.*]

KRISTINE: Really?

NORA: Do other people do that?

KRISTINE: No. I mean, I don't know. Why does he do that?

NORA: He thinks I'm no good with money. He thinks I waste it. Then
. . . for a while there I wasn't giving him my ATM receipts and he
never knew how much money was in our account and he bounced
some checks. I told him I lost them, but it kept happening so he
took away my card. But I wasn't losing them.

[*Small beat.*]

You can't tell Terry this—

KRISTINE: Something else I can't tell him?

NORA: No, he doesn't know this. But it's important to me that you
know, that I'm not some idiot and I'm not some spoiled little rich
girl. I'm actually very good with money. I've just had to do a lot of
juggling. Because I did something that involved a lot of risk. But I
had to do it. For Terry.

KRISTINE: What did you do?

NORA: I saved his life.

KRISTINE: How?

NORA: I paid for the rehab.

KRISTINE: I thought your father left you the money.

NORA: My father was broke. He didn't leave me anything. I came up
with the money. I borrowed it.

KRISTINE: Okay.

NORA: No you don't understand. We were in over our heads. We
couldn't even qualify to buy this place. No bank was going to loan
us anything.

KRISTINE: Then where'd you get it?

NORA: A certain individual loaned it to me. I'm paying it back, with interest.

KRISTINE: Who?

NORA: Nobody you know.

KRISTINE: How are you paying this thing off?

NORA: It's been hard. Once Terry took my ATM card, I tried skimming some off the top of the grocery money—like I bought stuff at Trader Joe's instead of Whole Foods, but Terry's really picky and it wasn't worth all the running around. And whatever he gives me for the kids I feel like I have to spend on them. So a lot of it comes from my stuff. Like, if he gives me money for clothes, I buy knock-offs and he doesn't know the difference. Everything looks good on me. Luckily. Except shoes. You can always tell cheap shoes.

KRISTINE: So you're never going to tell him?

NORA: Not until I'm old and ugly. Then if he thinks about trading me in for a new model he won't be able to. He'll owe me.

[KRISTINE *laughs.*]

You think I'm kidding but I'm not. I know how these things work.

[*She pats* KRISTINE's *knee.*]

Don't worry. Everything's going to be fine. Terry got his promotion. We can have fun again. We can have everything nice.

KRISTINE: It's nice now.

NORA: You should see—Terry's clients have these parties. Everything is real, you know? No Pottery Barn in sight. That's the curse of lawyers and bankers—you can see right into your clients' world but you can't touch a thing.

KRISTINE [*looking around*]: Well, even if it is Pottery Barn, it looks fine.

[*The phone rings.*]

NORA: I better get that.

[*She looks at the caller ID, hesitates, then answers it.*]

Hello? . . . This is a really bad time . . . Well there are people here . . .

[KRISTINE *makes a move to leave;* NORA *motions her to stay. Beat.*]

[*Nervously*] Why do you want to talk to him?

[*Beat.*]

Couldn't it wait until after the New Year? . . . Fine . . . Fine, I'll get him.

[*She knocks on the study door.*]

Terry? Phone.

[*She listens until* TERRY *picks up; then she hangs up.*]

[*Brightly*] I guess I'll have to get used to that. Everybody's going to want something from him now.

KRISTINE: I don't want to ask him about a job if he's being bombarded—

NORA: I didn't mean you.

[*The study door opens and* PETE *enters, carrying his CD case.*]

PETE: The guy's never off work. [*To* KRISTINE] Hi.

NORA: Pete, this is my friend Kristine Linde.

PETE [*overlapping with "Kristine"*]: The famous Kristine Linde. I've heard a lot about you.

KRISTINE: Oh yeah?

PETE: All good. The big sister Nora never had. [*To* NORA] It's so weird to me I didn't know you in college.

KRISTINE [*to* NORA]: You didn't know Terry in college?

NORA: We met at Taste of Chicago.

PETE: At the beer tent.

NORA: It's so cheesy. We never even go to Taste of Chicago anymore. No, Terry and Pete lived off campus in a swinging bachelor pad.

PETE: And Nora was always hanging out with those patchouli-soaked, artsy types.

NORA: No I wasn't.

KRISTINE [*overlapping*]: No she wasn't.

[*They laugh.*]

NORA: Kristine always gave me shit for pledging.

KRISTINE: Do your cheer.

NORA: No.

KRISTINE: It's so pathetic.

NORA: It's embarrassing.

PETE: C'mon. You do yours, I'll do mine.

NORA: Fine.

[*She stands up straight and does a cheer.*]

Chi-Os, Chi-Os, Chi-O Chi-Os are good!

[*Small beat.* KRISTINE *and* PETE *bust out laughing.*]

KRISTINE: That's what kills me. They're not great or outstanding. They're just good.

PETE [*overlapping*]: They're *good*. [*To* NORA] Did she know Raj?

KRISTINE: Raj Patel?

PETE: Terry's talking to him now.

KRISTINE: I heard he was making a fortune in some biotech start-up.

PETE [*to* KRISTINE]: Stem-cell research. It's fairly ingenious, actually. There are these IVF clinics that prescreen for hereditary diseases— they only implant the healthy embryos. So Raj is taking the leftover ones, the diseased ones, and developing new lines from them. Rebuilding the architecture of the disease to try and find a cure. There's huge potential in it.

KRISTINE: Wow.

PETE: Of course there's no federal funding, so he's got to raise every penny on his own.

KRISTINE: It's an amazing idea.

PETE: Raj was always smart. Weird though.

[PETE *walks to the kitchen.*]

[*Filling a glass with water*] Remember in school, he stole all that money from the Young Republicans—

KRISTINE: Nobody proved that.

PETE: But there was still something suspicious about him. He was always joining things. I don't like joiners.

NORA [*casually*]: Did you catch why he was calling?

PETE: He's in trouble, I guess. He's under investigation by the SEC.

NORA: He is? What for?

PETE: I don't know, but I guess he's hitting Terry up for another loan.

KRISTINE [*to* NORA]: Terry loaned him money?

NORA: The bank did. Yes. Terry mentioned that to me. Terry didn't approve the loan, of course. He just did the analysis. Then his boss made the final decision. But I believe that was the case. That Bank One loaned him money. Yes.

KRISTINE: Maybe we shouldn't be talking about this.

PETE: It's no secret. Raj has been all over town trying to drum up more investors. He must be desperate if he's calling Terry at home. On a Saturday.

NORA: Wait a minute . . . it's up to Terry whether or not he could get a loan?

PETE: Yeah.

NORA: I guess I knew that but I didn't *know* that. You know?

PETE: No.

NORA: Division Head. Oh wow. [*Thinking*] So Terry's going to have power over all these people? Oh, this is great!

[NORA *reaches into her purse.*]

Who wants a truffle?

PETE: Does Terry know you bought those?

NORA: Kristine brought them.

KRISTINE: I didn't—

NORA: She didn't know that Terry hates them.

KRISTINE: And why does he hate them?

PETE: He thinks they'll make her fat.

NORA: They're ten dollars. For a box of four.

KRISTINE: Oh. Well. What can I say? I'm an obscenely extravagant person.

NORA: No. Now and then you just like a wholesome treat. [*Pointing one out to* KRISTINE] That one's your favorite, right? Sweet curry and coconut.

[KRISTINE *takes it.*]

And here.

[NORA *hands one to* PETE.]

Candied violets in a chocolate ganache.

KRISTINE [*eating*]: Boy. This is almost worth some of what I paid for it.

NORA: See?

[NORA *picks up* PETE's *CD case.*]

This is nice. What is it? Ghurka?

PETE: Yeah.

NORA [*feeling it*]: I want some Ghurka. [*Grabbing* PETE] Oh, I want everything! Just tell Terry to give me everything!

PETE: Maybe you should lay off the chocolate.

NORA: But I love this chocolate. Hell, I could fuck this chocolate.

PETE: Interesting.

KRISTINE [*overlapping*]: Nora—

[TERRY *enters.* NORA *quickly hides the truffle box.*]

TERRY: You have to hand it to the guy. He is bold.

NORA: What'd you tell him?

TERRY [*to* KRISTINE]: Hello.

NORA: Oh, Terry, this is Kristine.

TERRY [*shaking* KRISTINE's *hand*]: Nice to meet you.

KRISTINE: You too.

NORA: Kristine Linde.

[*Small beat.*]

She was my R.A. Remember? I told you she was coming over.

TERRY: Oh, right.

NORA: I told Kristine about your promotion. She's really impressed.

KRISTINE: Yes. Congratulations.

NORA: Kristine was in transaction services at Arthur Andersen.

KRISTINE [*quickly*]: In Atlanta.

TERRY: Oh. That's rough.

NORA: So she's in the market for a job and I thought maybe the two of you could talk? Maybe you could share some of your expertise?

KRISTINE: I don't want to impose—

NORA [*putting a hand up to stop* KRISTINE, *as if to say she's working*]: I told her, that I know from personal experience, that the best person in the world to work under, is you.

TERRY: Did you now? Well in that case—

[TERRY *pulls out his wallet and reaches into it.*]

  [*To* KRISTINE] Why don't you send me a résumé?

[*He hands* KRISTINE *a card.*]

  I'll give it a look and see what I can do.

KRISTINE: That would be great. Thank you.

TERRY: No problem. [*To* NORA] We're going to get some wine.

NORA: So what did you tell him?

TERRY: Who?

NORA: Raj?

TERRY [*aware of* KRISTINE]: I told him I'd think about it.

KRISTINE: I think I'll walk out with you. I have to do some Christmas shopping myself.

TERRY: I hear soap is big this year.

NORA [*to* KRISTINE]: Come back for dinner.

KRISTINE: I'm afraid I can't. But thank you so much for everything. It's so good to see you.

[KRISTINE *gives* NORA *a big hug. She,* PETE, *and* TERRY *start putting on coats.*]

NORA: Next time you can meet the kids.

TERRY: It's freezing. You need a ride, Kristine?

[*They all head out through the back door. The following is off.*]

KRISTINE: Could you drop me off at the Red Line?

TERRY: No problem.

KRISTINE: Bye, Nora!

NORA: Bye!

[NORA *reenters and closes the back door. She takes the truffles back out and enjoys the last one all by herself. The front door opens, and* MARTA *enters with the three children.*]

My babies are home!

MARTA: We're home.

[*There is instant chaos as the kids enter, bundled in layers and layers of winter clothes.* MAX *and* MACEY *carry ice skates, and* SKYLER *carries skates and a hockey stick.* MARTA *has backpacks, stray scarves, and a round, plastic sled.* MARTA *and* NORA *move the kids inside, taking off coats and hats and gloves as they go. The following erupts and overlaps from the kids and* NORA. *Cries of "Hi Mommy!" "Where's Daddy?" come from the kids.*]

NORA: How was it?

[MARTA *helps the children take their boots off.*]

MARTA: Don't track.

[*The kids give reports, such as: "Max fell." "They didn't have the goals set up." "I need new skates."* MACEY *holds a tin of Altoids, which she shakes.*]

MACEY: These are vitamins. These are vitamins.

NORA: No, Macey. Those are Altoids.

[NORA *and* MARTA *get most of the stuff off the kids and leave it in a big heap.*]

MARTA [*looking through the stuff*]: I can't find Macey's hood—she wanted it off her coat.

SKYLER: Can we watch a DVD?

NORA: Don't you want to play with me?

[*The kids scream and then pile on top of* NORA, *on top of the coats. There is much hugging and tickling and screaming.*]

Oh you got me!

[NORA *is laughing with the children. Suddenly,* RAJ PATEL *is standing in the entryway. He watches* NORA *for a long moment; then she looks up and sees him.* MARTA *and the kids see him too. The kids are quiet.*]

SKYLER: Mommy, there's a strange man here.

RAJ: The door was open.

[NORA *stands up quickly.*]

NORA [*to the children*]: Skyler, sweetie—okay, guys? Guys? Go back in
    the TV room and pick out a DVD if you want. Go on.

[*The kids don't need prompting; they run off.* NORA *stands staring
at* RAJ.]

MARTA: You want me to go?

RAJ: Yeah.

NORA: It's okay, Marta, I know him. Why don't you go on back with
    the kids. I'll come play with them in a minute.

MARTA: Yell if you need me. I'll hear.

[MARTA *exits.*]

NORA: What are you doing here?

RAJ: I wanted to talk to you alone.

NORA [*pointing*]: Terry's in his office.

RAJ: I just saw him leave.

NORA: You're spying on us?

RAJ: Was that Kristine Linde? With Terry?

NORA: Yes.

RAJ: I thought it was. I remember her from college.

[*Small beat.*]

Anyway, I don't know what Terry told you—

NORA: He said you wanted a loan.

RAJ: Yes.

NORA: Is the SEC really after you?

RAJ: Where'd you hear that?

NORA: In the alumni magazine.

RAJ: Cute. That's cute.

NORA: Is it true?

RAJ: They investigate people all the time. It doesn't mean I've done anything.

NORA: Except steal from people.

RAJ: I'm trying to help people.

NORA: You wouldn't be calling Terry at home, on a Saturday, if you weren't desperate.

[*Beat.*]

RAJ: I'm having some trouble raising capital.

NORA: What did you do?

RAJ: I didn't do anything. I happen to be involved in a very . . . risky but potentially groundbreaking enterprise. But there's a lot of government regulation and the FDA is Byzantine in its machinations. So funding is difficult to come by. And maybe, when we made our public offering, my partners might have exaggerated our progress and maybe we didn't register some of our stock options with the SEC. And maybe I let the company buy me a Jaguar. Which, apparently, gave the wrong impression. So maybe some of our shareholders are planning to sue, but all of this can be remedied if I can raise two million dollars—

NORA: Two million dollars?

RAJ: Or a million, right now, as a short-term solution. We are this close—

[*He measures an inch with his fingers.*]

—to developing seventy different fully characterized stem-cell lines. The research possibilities are endless. Imagine, hereditary diseases that have destroyed lives for centuries—gone. Fragile X? Tay-Sachs? Thalassemia? Distant memories. And all that stands in the way is a million dollars—maybe a million five—but your husband won't give it to me.

NORA: It's a lot of money.

RAJ: It's chump change. He hands out ten times that without blinking an eye.

[*Small beat.*]

In six months I can prove this thing is real. But if we quit now, it won't be real, it'll be dust. All the research, everything, wasted.

NORA: Well I can't help you.

RAJ: That's funny. And ironic. Because I remember one time this woman came to me and she was really desperate for some money herself. And I loaned her a hundred thousand dollars—no questions asked—and she's been really bad about paying me back. Which would be fine, if I loaned it to her out of the goodness of my heart, to help a friend, blah blah blah—but I didn't. It was a business transaction. I expected something in return and now I'm calling in the favor.

NORA: I'm paying you interest—

RAJ: I expect her to use her influence with her husband. I'm sure she has some.

NORA: Of course I do.

RAJ: Then convince him to give me the money.

[NORA *doesn't answer.*]

Maybe I should tell him about our little arrangement—

NORA: Go ahead. As soon as he gets his bonus he'll write you a check.

RAJ: It's a little bit more complicated than that, don't you think?

NORA: He didn't approve your loan, he only did the analysis.

RAJ: He recommended the loan, Nora.

NORA: So?

RAJ: So? [*Amazed*] Does the word "kickback" mean anything to you?

[*Beat.*]

How about "scandal"? "Felony"? "Prison"?

NORA: You're crazy.

RAJ: Ask Terry! He'll tell you. There's a line. And when you cross that line, you're a thief. I should know. I still can't catch a break because everybody thinks I stole that money from the Young Republicans—

NORA: You did.

RAJ: Ten years ago!

[*Small beat.*]

> I can redeem myself. But I can't do it if you won't help me. And if you won't help me . . . [*sigh*] then I'm going to have to tell Terry what you did. And even if you don't know what you did, Terry will know. In a business based on reputation . . . one word from me . . .

[NORA *doesn't answer.*]

> I think you get the picture. If I'm going down, you're going with me. Talk to your husband.

[RAJ *exits through the front door.* NORA *stands, afraid. Then she absent-mindedly picks up some of the kids' clothes. She finds the hood from* MACEY's *jacket. It is small and lined with fur. She looks at it for a moment, stroking the fur.*]

NORA: Like a little bunny.

[*She comes to herself, drops the hood, and calls.*]

> Marta?!

MARTA [*off*]: What?

NORA: Can you . . . I need to talk to you.

[MARTA *enters.*]

MARTA: What?

NORA: Do me a favor, okay, and don't tell Terry that man was here.

MARTA: Okay.

NORA [*picking up an envelope*]: And here, I got you this gift card—so you get what you need with that.

MARTA: Okay.

NORA: Of course, that's not your real present. Your real present's a bonus. You'll get your real present later.

MARTA: Thanks.

NORA: Thank you, Marta. Thank you.

[MARTA *exits through the hall door.*]

Damn it! Okay. Stay calm.

[*She looks at the tree. Long pause.*]

[*Quietly*] I can fix this. I can fix it.

[NORA *goes to the tree and moves an ornament a few inches. She stares at it. She moves it again.*]

TERRY [*entering through the back door with a case of wine*]: Nora?

NORA: Hey! Where's Pete?

TERRY: Was somebody here?

NORA: No. Why?

TERRY: Nora, I saw Raj Patel leaving the house when I pulled up.

NORA: You did?

TERRY: Were you going to tell me?

NORA: I said I'd talk to you—

TERRY: What did he want?

NORA: To talk. To you. About that loan. He says he's this close to curing cancer. Or something.

TERRY: I can't believe he'd come over here and play on you! That's it. That decides it.

NORA: But can't you help him?

TERRY: No, I can't help him! The guy's in real trouble. If he'd just come clean with the SEC, they'd fine him. But if he tries to cover it up he'll end up in prison.

NORA: Prison?

TERRY: It's always the lying that gets people. It's called obstruction of justice, you know. Contempt of court.

[*He goes into his study, talking from there while he gets his laptop.*]

The original business model he presented us was good. I thought it was a good risk and I didn't want to hold all that college stuff against him since nobody ever proved anything. But only an idiot would loan him money now. [*Coming back in with the laptop*] I can't believe he came over here. You can't leverage a personal relationship like that—

NORA: I only listened.

TERRY: I know you have a big heart, but there's no wiggle room in this business. Remember that.

NORA: I will. I'm sorry.

TERRY [*more softly*]: And when I ask you something, you may as well tell me the truth. I always know when you're lying. You do this thing with your mouth.

NORA: I do?

TERRY: Right at the corners. It sort of freezes.

NORA: That's not very pretty.

TERRY: No.

[*He sits, opening the laptop.*]

NORA: I'm sorry. [*Nervously*] I guess I should get dinner started.

TERRY [*working on the computer*]: Look at this. Almost . . . thirty emails.

[NORA *lingers. She picks up soap and other purchases and starts putting them back into the bags.*]

NORA: Did you know New Year's Eve is going to be a costume party?

TERRY [*reading*]: Really?

NORA: I ran into Carol when I came home. Eighties theme.

TERRY: That's funny.

NORA: I wonder what I should be?

TERRY: You'll come up with something.

NORA: I can't think of anything good. Everything seems so dumb.

TERRY: We are talking the eighties.

NORA: Maybe you could help me think of something.

[TERRY *looks up.*]

TERRY: You're asking my advice?

NORA: I feel kind of dull lately.

TERRY: Okay. I'll put my thinking cap on.

[Beat. NORA *finishes packing up her purchases. She goes to the kitchen to start dinner.*]

NORA: I thought we'd have lamb.

TERRY: Sounds good.

[Beat. TERRY *and* NORA *both work.*]

> You know, the thing with Raj—is maybe it's having gone through rehab or something, but the thing that gets me is the lying. I almost have a physical reaction to it. You're an adult, you know? Take responsibility for yourself. Fess up and take your fucking lumps.

[NORA *keeps working.*]

> He's trying to blame everything on his partners but I'm like, "Buddy, you're in this up to your ears." There's no justification for this bullshit. I don't care if you are, theoretically, going to save lives. There's nothing noble about lying your ass off.

[Beat.]

> Pete says you had some of those truffles.

NORA: Kristine brought them.

TERRY: Lucky you.

[Lights go out.]

ACT 2

[*December 30. All the presents beneath the tree are gone except for a couple, unwrapped but still in their boxes. The sound of an electronic keyboard with a built-in drum machine being played randomly and loudly comes from the TV room. A pile of clothes is on the couch.* NORA *is sorting through them absently. The keyboard noise gets louder.*]

NORA [*to herself*]: Jesus Christ.

[*Yelling*] Skyler?! Macey?! Could you stop playing that please?

[*The keyboard stops, but the drum machine continues.*]

Find something quiet to play, okay? Mommy's trying to think.

[*The drum machine goes silent.* MARTA *enters carrying plates and empty cups from lunch. She heads toward the kitchen.*]

Marta, please, I have so much to do. Can't they draw or something? I got them that whole art set and they haven't touched it.

MARTA: They like that piano. They like the noise.

NORA: Sometimes I think Pete looks for the loudest toys. Last year he gave them that remote-controlled car, with the siren on it?

MARTA [*laughing*]: Oh yeah.

NORA: Terry finally threw it away.

MARTA: He gave it to me.

[MARTA *quietly goes into the kitchen and puts the dishes into the sink.* NORA *watches her.*]

NORA [*as* MARTA's *heading back to the TV room*]: Thanks for coming in today.

MARTA [*shrugging*]: If you need me, you need me.

NORA: I have so much to catch up on and I have to put together a costume for this stupid party.

MARTA: You look tired.

NORA: I feel like I work so much harder now than when I actually had a job.

MARTA: It probably just feels that way.

NORA: I don't know.

MARTA: You're not counting all the time on the train and stuff. Having a job's hard.

NORA: I couldn't stand to be away from the children all day.

MARTA: Yeah, that's hard.

[*Small beat.*]

NORA: I know you miss your children when you're here—

MARTA: It's okay.

NORA: I don't know how you do it, is all I'm saying.

MARTA: You try not to think about them. Because then you end up worrying. Like, this morning, Raven was crying because I gave her this My Little Pony salon for Christmas and you can shampoo and set the ponies' hair? And I promised her I'd play it with her today. But then I had to come in and work. So I'm wondering right now, you know, is she still going to be crying when I get home? Is she maybe going to open one of the My Little Pony shampoo bottles and maybe drink it and get sick? Or maybe worse, is she going to put one of the My Little Pony barrettes in her mouth and choke to death? Am I going to come home to find her all dead on the carpet? Stuff like that.

NORA: Does your sister still take care of her?

MARTA: My sister moved to Orlando. There's a lady down the street who does day care.

NORA: Do you think children forget their mothers, if they go away?

MARTA: Like, on vacation?

NORA: Or longer. Like, to the army or prison or something.

MARTA: You joining the army?

NORA: God no. I was just wondering if you could ever really forget your mother. Mine died, you know, when I was little, but I still remember her. I remember how she smelled. She wore Jean Naté and she smoked. I thought she died because she didn't like me. How stupid is that?

[NORA shakes her head.]

No, I can't go back to work. At least not until they're all in school. I have to find the money somewhere else.

MARTA: What money?

NORA [*laughing brightly*]: Money to live. We all need money to live.

MARTA: I guess that's how it's set up.

[*The doorbell rings.*]

NORA: Who's that?

MARTA: I'll get it.

NORA: Tell whoever it is we're not home. I can't talk to anybody.

MARTA: Okay.

[MARTA *exits to the front door.* NORA *nervously moves behind the tree. The door opens.*]

MARTA [*off*]: Nobody's home.

KRISTINE [*off*]: Oh that's okay. I just wanted to drop off some presents—

[NORA *moves from behind the tree.*]

NORA [*calling*]: It's Kristine! Marta? It's okay, it's Kristine.

[MARTA *reenters, followed by* KRISTINE *carrying two gifts: a box of cigars in a gift bag and a wrapped board game.*]

I thought you were a Jehovah's Witness.

[NORA *laughs. She and* KRISTINE *hug.*]

How was your Christmas?

KRISTINE: Good. I brought Terry a little thank-you present.

NORA: He said you had a good talk.

KRISTINE: He was very helpful. And I wanted to drop this off for the kids.

NORA: You really didn't have to.

MARTA: You want me to take it to them?

NORA: Let's let Kristine give it to them. Thanks, Marta.

[MARTA *nods and exits to the TV room.*]

NORA [*making sure* MARTA *is gone*]: I feel so bad, I had to call her in today, but I have so much to do. And it's all so silly. Sometimes I wonder why I went to college. [*Gesturing toward the pile of clothes*] The people upstairs are having a costume party tomorrow night with an eighties theme. I can't think of anything to be. I can't remember the eighties. A whole decade—and I don't even know what I was doing then.

KRISTINE: Growing up.

NORA: But what was I *doing*? I should have planned more for my life. Like you. I want Skyler to be like you. Independent.

[NORA *picks up a short, ruffly skirt.*]

Now what about this? It's kind of Madonna isn't it? With a rosary and some fishnet stockings? I could pull it off.

KRISTINE: You need some of those lace gloves—

NORA: With no fingers! Oh my God those were awful. Dr. Pete says I should be the *Flashdance* chick. I'd do it if I could find some leg warmers.

KRISTINE: Dr. Pete's a real charmer, isn't he?

NORA: What do you mean?

KRISTINE: He acted like he'd heard so much about me—the famous Kristine. And then Terry obviously had no idea who I was.

NORA: That's not true—

KRISTINE: I don't mind.

NORA: No, Pete's not lying. He has heard all about you. Terry just—he's a little jealous because he thinks I dated all these guys in college, so even when I mention things I did with girlfriends, he always assumes there was some guy lurking in the background. But Pete doesn't care. I can tell him anything.

KRISTINE: Is that who you borrowed the money from?

NORA: No.

KRISTINE: You said his practice was doing well.

NORA: At the time, it wasn't. At the time . . . Pete was sick, at the time. He had liver cancer.

KRISTINE: God.

NORA: They'd operate, but the tumors would come back and they were afraid it would spread. So he had a liver transplant. Just over a year ago. He was incredibly sick, before. So thin and lethargic. But he's doing great now.

KRISTINE: Good for him.

NORA: So I went somewhere else for the money and it's not a problem so don't worry about it, okay? [*Heading off*] Come on, let's go give the kids their present.

KRISTINE: It's Chutes and Ladders. I didn't know . . .

NORA: That's great! You can teach them how to play.

KRISTINE: Oh good.

[*It's not good.* NORA *and* KRISTINE *exit through the hall door.* TERRY *enters through the back door, dressed for work, carrying his computer case, a briefcase, and a stack of papers. He unburdens himself, setting down the cases and papers, taking off his overcoat, and unloading his cell phone and wallet on the dining-room table.*]

TERRY [*calling*]: Hello?

[*He looks at the clothes on the couch.*]

What is all this crap? [*Calling*] Nora?

NORA [*entering quickly*]: Hey!

[NORA *gives* TERRY *a long kiss.*]

TERRY: Hey. What's that for?

NORA: I missed you.

[NORA *takes off his tie.*]

I wish you could stay home this week.

TERRY: Too much to do. [*Gesturing to the clothes*] What's all this?

NORA: I'm still trying to pick out a costume. What are you going to be?

TERRY: Pete's lending me an XTC T-shirt.

NORA: That's so lame.

TERRY: That's so me. I'm going to get out of this suit.

[TERRY *heads toward the hall door.*]

NORA: Terry?

TERRY [*stopping*]: Yeah.

NORA: If I asked you to do something for me and I promised you I would do anything you wanted in return—anything at all—would you please, maybe, consider it?

TERRY: What is it?

NORA: I mean I would do anything at all.

[*She runs his tie through her fingers.*]

Nothing's too dirty.

TERRY [*grinning*]: I like it when No-No gets dirty.

NORA: Then say yes-yes to No-No.

TERRY: What's up?

NORA: Would you please just rethink this whole thing with Raj—

TERRY: Are you seriously bringing this up again?!

NORA: But maybe he's changed—

TERRY: Explain to me please why you're asking me this. What did you promise him?

NORA: Just that I would talk to you.

TERRY: But what? Why do you care?

NORA: Because.

[*Small beat.*]

I'm afraid of him. He seemed desperate. And desperate people will do anything.

TERRY: What could he possibly do?

NORA: I'm afraid he knows something.

[TERRY *waits.*]

[*Haltingly*] About the rehab, or the drugs. Maybe he'll tell somebody at the bank and then—what if you lost your job? We'd lose the house. We'd lose everything.

[*Small beat.*]

TERRY: Like your father did.

NORA: Yes.

TERRY: Well, I'm not your father. I'm in control of myself.

NORA: He was an alcoholic, not a murderer.

TERRY: He drove his company into the ground. He treated it like his own personal piggy bank. And all those people lost their jobs, because of his drinking.

NORA: Right. Well anyway, I don't want anything to happen to you because of your drug addiction.

[*Beat.*]

TERRY: When Jim told me about the promotion, I told him about the rehab. And he said he appreciated me telling him but the offer still stood. And that's what I mean when I say you have to tell the truth and take your lumps. Okay?

[*Beat.*]

NORA: I'm sorry.

TERRY: Do you still not trust me? Is that it?

NORA: I just get scared, sometimes.

TERRY: What can Raj do? Bad-mouth me? No one's going to listen to that guy. He's a loser and everybody knows it. Remember in college, he said his dad owned the Hyatt? Downtown? Turned out he owned a Patel Motel in fucking Dixon. The Dixon Budget Inn.

NORA: See? He'll lie about anything.

TERRY: Freshman year, you know, he lived down the hall from me? And Friday nights he was always sitting in his room watching *Star Trek: The Geek Generation*, and I felt sorry for the guy. So one night a bunch of us were going out drinking and I asked him to come along. No big deal, you know, but after that he thought we were best buds. I couldn't get rid of him. And then, out of nowhere, he starts calling me the T-Man. It was so embarrassing. That's half of why I moved off campus, was just to get away from the dillhole.

[*Small beat.*]

But the first time he came into the bank, it seemed like he'd changed. He seemed like a professional—and the guy's smart—everybody knows that. But then, when he gets the loan, I'm standing there, suit and tie, and I go to shake his hand, you know, "Glad it worked out." And he holds up his hand and says, "High five, T-Man." In front of the whole office. I could have killed him.

NORA: You're so petty.

TERRY [*angrily*]: The guy's got a shitty personality. And personality counts.

[*Beat.*]

You think I'm petty?

NORA: No.

TERRY: People judge you on appearance. Like the thing with the hair, there are studies. Equally qualified candidates, if one's fat and one's thin . . . A tall guy, a short guy. People don't always know they're doing it but they judge and they pick the tall, thin guy with hair. So it's not petty. It's my fucking career.

NORA: I know.

TERRY: And don't worry about Raj. I left him a message this morning and told him in no uncertain terms, he's not getting the loan and he is never to talk to you again.

NORA [*overlapping*]: Terry—!

TERRY: He's nothing to be scared of—

NORA [*overlapping*]: Call him back! Call him back and tell him you changed your mind.

[TERRY *takes a step back from her.*]

TERRY [*overlapping*]: It's like I'm talking to myself. Did you not hear a word I said?

NORA: Yes.

TERRY: Then stop insulting me. This is my job. It's what I do. I make these decisions.

NORA: But—

TERRY: End of discussion, Nora.

[*He waits for her to say something else, but she stops herself, backs off.*]

Thank you. Now I'm going to change—

[TERRY *sees* KRISTINE's *coat.*]

Is somebody here?

NORA: Kristine. She's playing with the kids.

TERRY: Tell her she doesn't have to butter us up. She's got the job.

NORA: Oh. Thank you.

TERRY: She'll make me money. She's sharp.

NORA: Thank you though, anyway.

TERRY [*pointing*]: We're taking that tree down tomorrow.

NORA [*disappointedly*]: Oh . . .

TERRY: No Christmas past New Year's. That's the rule.

[TERRY *exits through the hall door.* NORA *stands, uncertain.*]

NORA [*quietly*]: I'll get the money. Other people have money—

[*A snowball hits the window with a loud thump.* NORA *screams.*]

Aaah!

[*The back door opens and* PETE *enters.*]

You scared me.

PETE: I thought you saw me.

[PETE *takes the cigars out of the gift bag.*]

Cohibas.

NORA: Kristine brought them for Terry.

PETE [*handing* NORA *a CD*]: I brought you something.

[PETE *takes off his coat.*]

NORA: The soundtrack to *Flashdance.*

PETE: She's a welder by day and a stripper by night. But in her heart, she lives only to dance!

NORA [*picking up the skirt*]: But I thought I'd be Madonna.

PETE: Madonna sucks.

NORA: You're just threatened by her sexuality.

PETE: I'm threatened by her suckiness.

NORA: But I'd be so hot.

[NORA *holds the skirt up. She gives her hip a shake.*]

"Like a virgin. Touched for the very first time."

[*He looks at her.*]

What's the matter? Don't you think it'll fit?

PETE: Will you wear underwear?

NORA: Pete!

PETE: A man's gotta dream.

NORA: You dream of me?

PETE: All the time.

[PETE *heads for the kitchen, where he gets a glass of water.* NORA *watches him.*]

Where's Terry?

NORA: He's changing.

[PETE *brings the water into the dining area, puts it down, and heads for his coat. From a pocket, he gets a Ziploc bag with eight different pills in it.* NORA *watches him. Pause.*]

I'm glad you're here.

PETE: Why?

NORA: I'm always glad when you're here. You make me feel safe.

PETE: Really? I'm glad.

NORA: What are you going to be? For the party?

PETE: I have this old Gang of Four T-shirt. . . .

NORA: You guys can't just wear T-shirts.

PETE: Then I'll have to think.

[*He opens the bag of pills, then begins to take them, one by one.*]

I want something emblematic of the eighties. Something gross.

NORA: So many pills.

PETE: Yeah.

NORA: How long do you have to take them?

PETE: Until I die, basically.

NORA: But I thought . . . Doesn't your body eventually, like, welcome the liver?

PETE: Like, throw it a party?

NORA: You know what I mean.

PETE: You watch too many movies. You don't take the liver and run. You just buy yourself a few years. Until something else goes wrong.

NORA: Like what?

PETE: These pills I take—they suppress my immune system so my body won't reject the liver? But in exchange, they cause their own, special little form of cancer. It's the ultimate catch-22. Not to mention, I could kill myself tomorrow just by eating sushi.

[NORA *stares at* PETE. *He starts to explain.*]

When your immune system's suppressed—

NORA: You never told me any of this.

PETE: It's kind of a downer.

NORA: You can't die.

PETE: Everybody dies.

NORA: But not you. You're cured and we're going to grow old together.

PETE: Okay.

NORA: Pete!

PETE: Well it's all speculative. The living and the dying. It's all speculative, so don't worry about it.

[*Beat.*]

NORA: In other words, you don't know what will happen.

PETE: It's like buying on margin.

NORA: You could just as easily live to be a hundred.

PETE: I could strike it rich.

NORA: Okay then.

[*Beat.*]

PETE: So show me your non-Madonna options.

NORA [*picking up a sweater*]: Not that I like your idea, but I thought maybe I could do a Jennifer Beals thing with this. I'll wear it off the shoulder.

PETE: Won't you stretch the collar?

NORA: I got it at H and M. It's cheap. It's soft though, feel.

[*He feels the sweater.*]

See? Tell me what you think.

[*She takes off the sweater she's wearing. Underneath she's wearing a lacy bra. She puts on the other sweater.* PETE *watches the whole time.*]

Then I pull it down like this . . .

[*She pulls the collar down off one shoulder and sees her bra strap.*]

I should take off the bra, though.

[NORA *unhooks her bra and pulls it out from beneath the sweater.*]

PETE: How do you do that?

NORA: We learn it at birth.

[NORA *drops the bra on the sofa, next to him. She models.*]

Yes or no?

PETE [*regarding her*]: What are you up to today?

NORA: Nothing. Why?

PETE: You're being very . . . cute.

NORA [*laughing*]: I may have a little of the devil in me.

PETE: You might at that.

[*Small beat.*]

[*Without looking at her*] If I didn't know better I'd say you were flirting with me.

[*Pause.*]

NORA: I want to ask you for something but I don't know how to do it.

PETE: What is it?

NORA: If I needed help, you would help me, wouldn't you?

PETE: Of course. Why would you doubt that?

NORA: I don't always know if you like me. You tease me so much.

PETE: Nora, Terry and I ran out of stuff to talk about ten years ago. I don't come over here to see Terry. I come to see you.

NORA: You do?

[*Small beat.*]

PETE [*tentatively*]: I don't know. Sometimes it seems like you have more fun with me.

NORA: I do. Sometimes. I mean, I love Terry. But there are the people you love, and then there are the people you want to be with.

PETE: Shouldn't you want to be with the people you love?

NORA: I am with the person I love.

PETE [*taking* NORA's *hand*]: Sometimes I wonder if you have any idea how beautiful you are.

NORA: Pete—

PETE: It's not just your face or your hair or those amazing lips—

NORA: Pete—

PETE: You have a beautiful heart. I've loved you for a long time, Nora.

[*He tries to kiss her.*]

NORA [*pushing him away, quietly but urgently*]: Oh God. No. Stop it. Stop it.

PETE [*going after her*]: He treats you like crap.

[*She pushes him away again.*]

NORA [*still quietly but urgently*]: That's not what I meant! Stop it! Pete. Don't!

[*She pulls away, gets up, and takes two steps back.*]

Stop it. That wasn't what I wanted.

PETE: Then what did you want?

NORA: I can't now. I'm sorry.

PETE: I'll do anything you want.

NORA: Shut up.

[TERRY *enters in jeans and a sweatshirt. He's aware something's wrong, but he's casual.*]

TERRY: Hey. What's going on?

NORA [*quickly pulling out the short skirt*]: We're having a fight so you have to decide this. I say Madonna but Pete says *Flashdance*.

[TERRY *looks at* PETE, *who is visibly upset.*]

TERRY: You're really fighting about this?

NORA: It's just he's so pushy.

PETE: And she's so obtuse.

TERRY: You're both crazy.

[TERRY *picks up a game disc.*]

[*To* PETE] Look what Nora got me. Death Match Four. I'm taking you on.

PETE: Yippee.

TERRY [*to* NORA]: You might want to rescue Kristine. Her eyes are glazing over. [*To* PETE] You nonbreeders are weak.

PETE [*heading off to the TV room*]: Weak and beaten.

[TERRY *stays behind.*]

TERRY [*to* NORA]: Is he okay?

NORA: He said he didn't feel well. He takes so many pills.

TERRY: I can't think about it without gagging.

[*The doorbell rings.*]

NORA: I'll get it. It's UPS.

TERRY: What'd you get?

NORA [*heading toward the front door*]: I exchanged those pants you
    ordered. I'll get it.

TERRY: Thanks.

[TERRY *exits through the hall door.* NORA *waits to make sure he is gone.
The doorbell rings again.*]

NORA [*yelling*]: I got it!

[NORA *almost runs to the door; she opens it.*]

   [*Off*] Terry's not home.

RAJ [*entering with* NORA]: I got his message. This isn't going to fly.

NORA: Why don't you go to a loan shark or something?

RAJ: That's really going to help me with the SEC.

[*He looks at her.*]

I guess I'll have to tell him.

NORA: He already knows, and he doesn't care.

RAJ: He doesn't know. If he knew he'd cave, he'd cave in a heartbeat.

NORA: No he wouldn't.

RAJ: Did you know? On his dorm-room door? Instead of his name the guy actually wrote, THE T-MAN?

NORA: That's not true.

RAJ: He's a tool.

NORA: Shut up! You can't talk about him like that.

RAJ: Fine. We don't have to talk.

[*He takes a Blackberry out of his pocket.*]

NORA: What are you doing?

RAJ: I'm going to send your better half an email. Outlining our little transaction . . .

NORA [*pulling on his arm*]: No no no. You can't!

RAJ: I even scanned the promissory note and made an attachment.

NORA: No! You don't understand. He'll kill me. He'll kill me.

RAJ: Terry? He'd never do that. That's illegal.

NORA: He'll take the whole thing on himself. He'll go—he'd work at a Seven Eleven before he'd do anything wrong, and I'll want to be dead, at that point. I'll kill myself.

[*They stop. She gets the idea just as* RAJ *does.*]

RAJ: Oh no. You don't have the guts.

NORA: How do you know?

RAJ: How would you do it? Jump? That'd leave a splatty mess. Pills? Often involve a lot of vomit. Gun to the head? Again, with the mess and the blown-out skull. You could drown yourself, but when they finally dragged you out of the river in the spring, you'd be all bloated and rotten and bald.

NORA: Fuck you.

RAJ: I'm sorry. But it's hard when you're at the mercy of a bunch of imbeciles. Just because you don't have any money.

NORA: But isn't your family rich? I thought your father owned the Hyatt. Downtown.

[Beat.]

RAJ: You grow up in Dixon, Illinois, with a name like Rajeshkumar Patel and see what it does to you. My dad busted his ass at that fucking Budget Inn—my mom cleaned toilets at the fucking Budget Inn just to send me and my sisters to school and I am not letting them down. Someday, somewhere, I'm buying them a Hyatt and they're going to live in the entire thing—a different room every day. And they'll watch TV all night at top volume and leave wet towels on the floors and never be out by noon.

NORA: Give me a week.

RAJ: You've had your chance.

NORA: But tomorrow's New Year's Eve.

RAJ: Midnight tomorrow. Makes a nice deadline. Tell Terry he has until then to get me the money.

[RAJ hits the "send" button on his Blackberry.]

Otherwise, there will be fireworks at the Helmers'.

NORA: You didn't just—

RAJ: Message sent.

[RAJ *looks at his Blackberry.*]

Don't you love modern technology?

NORA: Take it back.

RAJ: Terry knows where to reach me.

[NORA *looks to* TERRY'S *computer on the table.*]

NORA: Get it back!

RAJ [*shrugging*]: I can't. Good luck, Nora.

[*He exits through the entryway; the front door opens.* NORA *grabs the computer.* KRISTINE *enters from the TV room just as the front door closes.*]

KRISTINE: Raj? Nora, was that Raj?

NORA [*looking for some place to hide the computer*]: Shhhh! Please, Kristine. Terry can't know he was here.

KRISTINE: That's who you borrowed the money from.

NORA: Terry can't know. He hates Raj.

KRISTINE: Isn't he Terry's client?

NORA: I'm going to fix it. I'm going to find the money and I'm going to fix it.

KRISTINE: Ah boy. It was a kickback.

NORA: Help me hide this. I have to hide it.

[NORA *doesn't know where to put the computer.*]

I'm such an idiot, Kristine. I'm such a fucking idiot!

KRISTINE: Calm down.

NORA [*starting to panic*]: But I didn't know what to do! All I wanted was to be happy and be pregnant and happy.

[NORA *points at the portrait.*]

I wanted that portrait so bad but we couldn't afford it. So I went to get this belly mask instead—there's this woman who does a papier-mâché cast of your belly when you're pregnant and then she paints it however you want it and I thought at least I could do that. And she asked what I wanted on it and I stood there and tried to think of something nice but all I could think was, "Like what? A picture of my father dying? Or my husband on drugs? Or maybe the whole family in bankruptcy court?" So finally I said we were naming the baby Skyler, maybe something in the sky? Like a butterfly?—which—I don't give a shit about butterflies—but two weeks later she comes by with this bright blue mask with this big purple butterfly on it. It was hideous. As soon as she left I took it out into the alley and smashed it into pieces because I thought, "This is ugly and I don't want to remember any of this!" And one day I went to see Terry at the bank and Raj was in the lobby and I said, "How are you doing?" and he said, "I'm doing great," and he asked me was I doing okay and I wasn't. I needed money. And he didn't even ask *why*, he just *offered*. He offered and nobody else had offered. Nobody else ever offered anything!

[NORA *stops.*]

And I knew it was wrong and I didn't care! Terry wouldn't let me tell anybody how sick he was, so nobody could help. And Terry knows that. He'll think it's his fault and he'll take all the blame himself, but you can't let him. If anybody finds out, you tell them I knew exactly what I was doing and Terry didn't know anything about it. If he says he did, he's lying. Even though he never lies, he's lying.

[NORA *puts the computer on the table. She starts opening the case.*]

I'll delete it. What do I need? A password?

KRISTINE: Okay. Maybe I should talk to Raj.

NORA: Don't bother! You can't do anything.

KRISTINE [*getting her coat*]: There was a time when he would have listened to me. Maybe . . . I don't know. Maybe it's worth a shot. I'll see if I can catch him.

NORA [*pushing* KRISTINE *toward the front door*]: Tell him I'll come up with the money, I just need more time.

KRISTINE: Okay.

[KRISTINE *exits.* NORA *runs back to the computer and opens it, but she hears voices and quickly shuts it again.* TERRY *and* PETE *enter, mid-conversation.* NORA *quickly begins picking up clothes.*]

PETE: I would listen to Kenny Rogers. I would listen to Pink Floyd *post*–Roger Waters before I'd listen to the Eagles.

TERRY: Okay, I get it. You hate the Eagles.

[TERRY *goes to pick up his computer.*]

NORA: What are you doing? Weren't you playing your game?

TERRY [*picking up the computer*]: Pete kept killing me. We're going to finish burning that CD.

NORA: You can't. You promised me you'd help me with this costume and I still don't know what to wear.

TERRY: Wear a garbage bag. Go as a homeless person.

NORA: No. You promised me. Terry. Please. You stare at the computer all day.

[*She takes the computer from him and sets it down.*]

Now I could do Madonna—

PETE: Madonna was a whore.

NORA: Or I could do *Flashdance.*

[NORA *strikes a pose.* TERRY *picks up the computer again.*]

TERRY: It's a sweater.

NORA [*taking the computer from* TERRY *and putting it down*]: You have to get the whole effect. I'll do the dance.

TERRY: Seriously?

NORA [*going to the stereo*]: All you have to do is vamp.

[*She puts on the* Flashdance *CD.*]

TERRY: I loved this movie.

NORA: Watch and tell me how this looks.

[*"Maniac" blares from the stereo. She puts her head down like Jennifer Beals in the movie and starts stepping in place to the beat. She tosses her hair back.*]

Because I want to look good.

[TERRY *watches her for a moment.*]

TERRY: Wait. You want the full effect.

[*He reaches up and pulls her sweater down off her shoulder.*]

There. Now that's actually kind of sexy.

[*She dances the "Maniac" dance—as much as she can—from memory.* TERRY *watches, amused, then gives her a hand. He goes to pick up the computer again. She sees.*]

NORA: No no no.

[NORA *takes his hand and leads him to sit on the couch. She starts a new dance, a sort of lap dance. She begins dancing in front of him, turning and moving her hips like a stripper. He grins wider.* PETE *watches. She moves toward him, sexy. The music is loud.* KRISTINE *enters. She stands in the entryway, in her coat, and watches.*]

Here comes the good part.

[NORA *gyrates and turns, then she starts to inch her sweater up over her head.* TERRY *quickly stands.*]

TERRY: Nora.

PETE: She's not wearing a bra.

KRISTINE: What the hell?

[NORA, TERRY, *and* PETE *all turn and see* KRISTINE.]

TERRY [*pulling* NORA's *sweater down*]: Nora, stop.

NORA [*laughing*]: I'm just kidding. I'm not going to take my clothes off in front of Dr. Pete.

PETE: You know what? I gotta go.

[*He grabs his coat.*]

TERRY: Hey—we'll see you tomorrow night, right?

[PETE *exits.*]

TERRY [*heading for the stereo*]: Okay. I think we've had enough of this.

NORA [*swinging her hair around, stripper style*]: But I'm a maniac!

TERRY: You sure are.

[TERRY *is at the stereo. While his back is turned,* NORA *goes to* KRISTINE.]

NORA [*in a whisper that the audience may not hear*]: Did you find him?

[*The music stops.*]

KRISTINE: No.

[TERRY *turns. Beat.* NORA, TERRY, *and* KRISTINE *all stand still.*]

TERRY: Kristine. Can I take your coat?

KRISTINE: Oh no, I just . . . I forgot to tell Nora, I can babysit tomorrow night if you need me.

NORA: What?

KRISTINE: Marta was telling me there's a big party in her neighborhood. I'd hate for her to miss it and I don't have anything to do.

NORA: She never told me.

KRISTINE: So I'll come by around eight?

TERRY: That's really nice of you, Kristine. Thanks so much.

KRISTINE: No problem. [*To* NORA] And don't forget to give Terry his cigars. See you guys tomorrow.

[*She exits.*]

TERRY [*looking at the cigars distractedly*]: Cohibas. Nice.

[TERRY *puts the cigars down.*]

So what was going on with you and Pete?

NORA: Nothing.

TERRY: Then why is your bra on the couch?

NORA: Nothing happened. I was trying stuff on and he came in and I didn't know it. He watched me for a minute and when I realized, I yelled at him.

[*Small beat.*]

He was very embarrassed.

TERRY: You shouldn't torture him like that.

NORA: I'm sorry.

TERRY: Because you, my dear . . .

[*He picks up his computer.*]

Well let's just say you're very attractive.

NORA: You're going to start this new job and we'll never have any time together.

[*Beat.*]

TERRY: When you said before that you'd do anything, no matter how dirty . . . did you mean that?

NORA: If you promise me one thing.

TERRY: What?

NORA: Promise me you won't work until after the New Year.

TERRY [*looking at* NORA]: Take off your sweater.

NORA: What if the kids come in?

TERRY: Then let's take a nap.

NORA: Put that down.

[NORA *takes the computer from him and kisses him. He kisses her back. Then he runs his hands up under her sweater.*]

TERRY: Pete wishes he could get his hands on these.

NORA: Terry . . .

TERRY: Come on.

[*They start to exit.* NORA *stops.*]

NORA: Don't we need music?

TERRY: No.

[*He takes her hand and leads her off toward the hall door. She looks back over her shoulder at the computer, almost wanting it.*]

[*Sternly*] Nora.

[*She relents. They exit. Lights fade.*]

ACT 3

[*The following night—New Year's Eve—a little before midnight. The party can be heard going on upstairs.* KRISTINE *and* RAJ *stand just inside the entryway.* RAJ *still wears his coat and hat.* KRISTINE *has just let him in. She holds a book she was reading, with a pen marking her place.*]

RAJ: Long time no see.

KRISTINE: Thanks for coming.

RAJ: I only came to collect.

KRISTINE: So you're going to go through with this?

RAJ: Why'd I have to meet you here?

KRISTINE: I'm babysitting.

RAJ: I thought you hated kids.

KRISTINE: Just because I don't want children doesn't mean I hate kids.

RAJ: Are they upstairs?

KRISTINE: Don't go up there.

[RAJ *listens to the party.*]

RAJ: I told her she had until midnight. I liked the thought of ruining Terry's New Year's.

KRISTINE: What do you have against them, exactly?

RAJ: It's that leader-of-the-pack thing. The alpha male breeds with the alpha female—instinctively, to keep the species strong. The only hope somebody like me has, is that one day I can design a killer robot to capture and enslave them.

KRISTINE [*regarding* RAJ]: You haven't changed a bit.

RAJ: I've had no motivation to change. You change to win someone's love. I had no love to win. The woman I loved told me I was worthless and irredeemable and left me with no hope.

KRISTINE: I never said you were worthless.

[*Small beat.*]

And I didn't want to live in a basement apartment for the rest of my life. I didn't want to sleep on some futon you found in the alley and come home to find you in sweatpants, watching *People's Court* and eating Froot Loops.

RAJ: You know, a year ago I was worth three million dollars, on paper. I thought about calling you. I thought about telling you, "I'm rich now"—but . . .

KRISTINE: What?

RAJ: I've had a lot of people turn on me in my life, but I didn't think you'd be one of them.

KRISTINE: I didn't think I was helping you by staying. I thought . . . the fact that I loved you somehow allowed you to be a jerk—I thought if I left, if I said, "No more," you'd look around and realize that you had to get off your ass and make something of yourself, and you did—

RAJ: Except I fucked it up—

KRISTINE: Couldn't you come clean with the SEC, pay your fines—

RAJ: Declare bankruptcy, restructure, rebuild, blah blah blah . . . Soon we'll have a president who isn't a religious retard. There'll be government funding again and nobody will need to buy from me.

KRISTINE: But isn't that a good thing?

RAJ: How?

KRISTINE: For people with, say, . . . diabetes?

RAJ: Well sure, if you want to get all human about it—

KRISTINE: Why can't you work for a not-for-profit?

RAJ: Please.

KRISTINE: Work for the greater good. Does it all have to be about money?

RAJ: Isn't that why you left me? Because I didn't have any money?

KRISTINE: I left you because you couldn't be honest about who you were.

[*Small beat.*]

Because you always wanted to impress the wrong people. I don't care about money. All I want is a respectable life—

[RAJ *snorts.*]

RAJ: Respectable.

KRISTINE: A life that I can respect with people I can respect and who respect me. Not some petty criminal. You were a petty criminal and you still are.

RAJ: This stuff with the SEC is technical bullshit—

KRISTINE: Blackmail is not technical bullshit.

[*Pause.* RAJ *looks away, guilty.*]

RAJ: See? You never should have left me. You were the only conscience I ever had.

KRISTINE: You've always had a conscience. But you need somebody around to remind you it's there.

RAJ: You could have done that.

KRISTINE: Maybe.

[*Small beat.*]

When I lost my job I had all this money saved up and I thought, "I'll travel, I'll reward myself." And I went to Europe, to London and then France and Italy, and 'round about week six I'm taking a boat around Lake Como and I'm looking at this amazing view. Every little town is like a clearer Xerox of the last one. These blues and yellows that could make your heart stop. And as I stood there, I thought to myself, "If the exchange rate in England was a buck fifty to the pound, then that cappuccino I had at the National Portrait Gallery cost me almost eight dollars—in billing hours that's not that much, but still . . ."

[*She trails off. Then she loses it.*]

[*Stop-starting*] And then I actually felt like I was going to vomit. I've been thinking crap like that for ten years—do you know—I have had the most profoundly meaningless life on the planet! Endless, inane conversations with business people who're so puffed up—me too, I guess—you have to convince yourself that what you do is earth-shatteringly important, because otherwise, you'd be forced to face the fact that you're spending seventy-five percent of your waking hours on utter crap. There'd be mass suicides, people in industrial parks everywhere would blow their brains out—so the only reason to do it, the only reason to punch the clock is if you're doing it *for* somebody. For somebody else so you can have a life with somebody else—if you're taking care of somebody else. Somebody you love. And I thought, "Who have I ever loved?—besides my parents of course—but who?"

[*Small beat. This is difficult for her.*]

So I moved to Chicago. Because I think, if we had been together this whole time, if we had been working for each other this whole time, then maybe we'd be further along. We wouldn't be spinning our wheels like this. I was hoping we could start over together. And I could help you this time. And we could do it together.

[*Beat.*]

Please don't laugh at me.

[*Pause.*]

RAJ: I admit, I'm torn here. Even though this gives me the upper hand, I'm forced to say that I very much want what you say to be true. But I also suspect it isn't—

KRISTINE: Why not?

RAJ: Because your little freshman charge is in trouble and I think you'd do whatever it takes to help her.

KRISTINE: No I won't. I want Terry to find out about the loan. I want Nora to get up off her knees.

RAJ: He doesn't know?

KRISTINE: She's kept him off the computer.

RAJ: She's very talented.

[RAJ *thinks.*]

Maybe I could hack into it somehow, delete it.

KRISTINE: No, I want him to know. I came in here yesterday and she was dancing? Or stripping? Whatever it was, it has to stop. I've never in my life seen so much insanity over thirty thousand dollars.

RAJ: A hundred thousand.

KRISTINE: She said rehab costs thirty.

RAJ: Rehab? Was it Terry's?

KRISTINE: These people live like children. I don't think anything in this house is paid for. And look at this—

[*She picks up one of the framed pictures.*]

There are wedding pictures everywhere! It's sick!

[*He looks at her and smiles.*]

RAJ: Look at you. You never cared what other people wanted. You only wanted what you wanted.

[*Small beat.*]

I've missed you.

KRISTINE: I've missed you, too.

[*From upstairs the noise increases, then people can be heard counting down to midnight: "Ten, nine, eight . . ."*]

You should go. They'll be home soon. Do you have the original note?

RAJ: At home.

KRISTINE: I'll meet you there.

RAJ: You know where I live?

KRISTINE: I kind of looked you up in the book.

RAJ: Listen, my place is a mess . . .

KRISTINE: I don't care.

RAJ: You really . . . you're making me feel . . . you know . . . happy.

[KRISTINE *smiles and kisses him.*]

KRISTINE: Happy New Year.

[*Noise comes from upstairs.*]

Now go.

[*He exits.* KRISTINE *packs up her things, gets her coat. She pulls a scarf from a sleeve, getting everything ready to put on. The back door opens and* TERRY *enters, gently pulling* NORA *in behind him.* NORA *is dressed like Jennifer Beals in* Flashdance. *She's wearing tight leggings and an off-the-shoulder sweatshirt. Her hair is bigger, and she's got on lots of makeup, but the effect is pleasing, in a tawdry way.* TERRY *is dressed as Ronald Reagan in a tuxedo, and he is carrying a rubber Reagan mask. He's been drinking.*]

NORA: Let's go back up. I wanted to stay.

TERRY: Nuh-uh. We made a deal. It's past midnight.

NORA: Please? I was having so much fun.

TERRY: We'll have fun. Right here.

[*He pulls her inside, starts to pull her to him.* KRISTINE *stops him by calling loudly.*]

KRISTINE: How was the party?

TERRY [*straightening up*]: You're still in one piece! Listen, thanks so much for watching the kids—

KRISTINE: My pleasure.

[*She starts putting on her coat and so on.*]

TERRY: Let me walk down to the corner and I'll get you a cab—

NORA: But Kristine needs some champagne—

KRISTINE: No I don't.

TERRY [*overlapping*]: She's probably tired—

NORA: But you didn't get to celebrate New Year's.

KRISTINE: It's fine, really. I'm going to get going.

TERRY: That's right.

[TERRY *picks up* KRISTINE'*s book.*]

Is this yours?

KRISTINE: Yes.

TERRY: You shouldn't read in this light. It's bad for your eyes.

KRISTINE: I don't mind.

TERRY: You gotta watch out. If you squint too much, those wrinkles over your nose will get deeper.

NORA: Terry . . .

TERRY [*rubbing* NORA'*s forehead between her eyebrows*]: You want to have skin like Nora's. Smooth as a baby's. She doesn't worry and she doesn't scowl.

KRISTINE: Nora's very pretty.

TERRY: Thanks.

KRISTINE: And I like to read.

[*Small beat.*]

If you don't mind getting me a cab, I'd appreciate it.

TERRY: Sure. No problem.

[*He grabs a coat and exits through the front door.*]

NORA [*as soon as* TERRY'*s gone*]: Did he come?

KRISTINE: I couldn't talk him out of it.

NORA: What am I going to do? I can't get into his computer. He's got it set up with this password—I tried the kids' names and mine— anything I thought he'd care about.

KRISTINE: You need to tell Terry the truth.

NORA: I can't!

KRISTINE: Then I don't know what I can do for you, Nora. I'm sorry.

NORA: Can't you stay?

TERRY [*off*]: Kristine? I think I got one!

[KRISTINE *takes up her bag.*]

NORA: Is Raj coming back?

KRISTINE: I'm sorry.

NORA: Will he call?

[*A cab honks, off.*]

TERRY [*off*]: Kristine?

[KRISTINE *hastily kisses* NORA *on the cheek.*]

KRISTINE: Good luck, Nora. I really am rooting for you.

[KRISTINE *exits.*]

NORA: Kristine?

TERRY [*off*]: Good night!

[*The front door closes. He enters.*]

    Thank God. She's so boring. [*Taking off his coat and throwing it on the sofa*] What was with Pete tonight?

NORA [*taking off her wig*]: What do you mean?

TERRY: He was really hitting the booze. I thought he wasn't supposed to drink.

NORA: I don't know. Aren't you tired?

TERRY: I feel great.

NORA: I'm tired.

TERRY [*going to her*]: See? It's a good thing we left.

[TERRY *looks at her.*]

I like that outfit.

NORA: It's silly.

TERRY: It's hot. I was watching you all night.

NORA: Well you weren't talking to me.

TERRY: I like watching people watch you. I pretend like I don't know you. I pretend we're strangers and all these guys want you. But I'm the only one who gets you. I leave with the prize.

NORA: I'm not a prize.

TERRY: You know what I mean. I like to pretend we've never done it before. [*Touching her hip*] I like these little legging things. What do you wear under them?

NORA [*turning away*]: A thong.

TERRY: Can I see?

NORA: I'm really tired.

[TERRY *picks up the Reagan mask.*]

TERRY: Let me see if I can put this better as the Great Communicator.

[TERRY *puts on the mask. He slips his finger into the waist of her leggings.*]

Mommy, show me your thong.

NORA [*pushing his hand away*]: Wrong president.

TERRY: Mr. Gorbachev? Tear down this wall!

[TERRY *pulls her to him. He runs his hand over her rear end, then pulls her pelvis to his.*]

So you're basically naked under there? Dirty girl—

NORA: I don't want to do that again.

[NORA *tries to push* TERRY *away, but he won't let her.*]

I don't want to, okay?

TERRY: You might as well give in. I'm bigger than you.

[*He tries to undress her, but she's really fighting hard.*]

NORA: Let go. Let me—GET OFF!

[*He releases her, steps back.*]

Take off that stupid mask.

TERRY [*taking it off*]: Okay. Jesus.

NORA: I don't want to, okay?

TERRY: What's wrong with you tonight?

NORA: Nothing. I—

[*A knock on the back door is heard.*]

Shit.

TERRY: Who's that?

[*The door opens and* PETE *enters, very drunk. He's dressed like Pee-wee Herman.*]

Hey Pee-wee. What's up?

PETE: I'd been waiting all night for somebody to say they loved something. You know? All night. And finally somebody said, "I love this salmon," and I said, "Why don't you marry it?"

TERRY: How're you getting home?

PETE: I didn't get to say Happy New Year's. Happy New Year's.

TERRY: How 'bout I call you a cab?

PETE: Wait. We gotta kiss.

[PETE *grabs* NORA, *who tries to get away, and plants one on her mouth.*]

That's for you.

[PETE *grabs* TERRY, *plants one on his mouth.*]

And that's for you.

TERRY: Okay there—

PETE: I'd kiss myself but . . . Hey! I'll kiss my own sorry ass.

[*He tries to kiss his ass, stumbles.* TERRY *catches him.*]

TERRY: Careful . . .

PETE: Hey. Have you got any of those cigars? The Cubans?

TERRY: You want one?

PETE: The Cuban Cohibas?

TERRY: Okay. One for the road.

[*He heads into his study.*]

PETE: You know, your wife is one hell of a dancer.

TERRY [*off*]: She is, huh?

PETE: She dances like that—what was that chick's name? The one that asked for John the Baptist's head? On a plate?

TERRY [*reentering with the box of cigars*]: Enjoying the libations tonight, are we?

PETE: Salome and the dance of the deadly veils.

[*Beat. They all stare at one another.*]

TERRY [*holding out the box to* PETE]: Cigar?

PETE: I do believe I shall.

[*He takes a handful, putting all but one in his pocket.*]

TERRY: Whoa.

PETE: Consider it your parting gift to the studio audience. Tonight, I bid you all farewell.

[PETE *bites the end off a cigar, spits it on the floor.*]

Nora? Could you do me the honor of honoring me with a light?

NORA: Terry, call him a cab.

[*She takes matches from a box on the table, lights the cigar.*]

TERRY [*picking up the phone*]: We'll get you home so you can get some sleep. We got some serious football to watch tomorrow.

[NORA *and* PETE *regard each other for a moment.*]

PETE: This is it. I bid you farewell, good-bye for good.

[PETE *takes a deep puff.*]

I'm not taking your crap anymore.

TERRY: What?

PETE: You're a bad influence, you know it?

TERRY: No.

PETE: With your pectorals and your—you get white goopy stuff in your eyes. Sleep in your eyes from your face mask or whatever you wipe on your face—your man cream—your rich man cream—

TERRY [*stopping him*]: Okay, you're drunk and I'm tired . . .

PETE: Your wife came on to me.

TERRY: What?

NORA [*overlapping*]: I did not!

PETE: On the couch, she was like, "Oh give it to me"—

NORA: I didn't!

PETE: Yes you did. Tease.

TERRY [*overlapping, taking* PETE's *arm*]: I'm not listening to this shit. Come on. Get out.

PETE: Grabber. She's a grabber.

[PETE *pulls free.*]

There's a world out there! There's a world of people with nothing, and a war going on. People's arms and legs getting blown off, people dying . . . and you two sit in here with, like, . . .

[*He picks up an elaborate tea-light candleholder, knocking the candles everywhere.*]

"I want this, gimme this. Gimme some Ghurka"—

[PETE *drops the candleholder.*]

NORA: Pete!

PETE: The earth could be colliding—on a direct collision course into the sun and [*indicating* NORA] you'd be like, "Poor me, where can I get some basil paste, where can I get a . . . a spooge infusion for the twat over there"—

TERRY [*grabbing* PETE]: Shut it!

[*The following overlaps as they struggle.*]

PETE [*grabbing* TERRY *back*]: You shut it! You stink! With your fucking—Old Spice—

NORA: Stop it!

PETE: C2 Tommy Hilfinger—

TERRY: Stupid—

PETE: Faggot stink—!

TERRY: Fuck you!

[*He finally pushes* PETE *hard.* PETE *stumbles backward, falls down.*]

PETE [*overlapping*]: You fucking—OW!

TERRY: Get up. Get out of here!

[PETE *crabs backward away from* TERRY.]

Take your fucking—

[TERRY *picks up a vase or a lamp.*]

—bullshit and your hard-on for my wife and get the fuck out of my house!

[PETE *holds his hands up, surrendering. Then he rises, slowly.*]

PETE [*upset*]: You should be nicer to me.

[PETE *makes his way to the front door, unsteadily.*]

The cold war is won. Remember the *Maine*. Freedom is on the march.

TERRY: Jesus.

PETE: Sic semper tyrannis.

[PETE *stops, turns to* NORA.]

Thank you, Nora. For the light.

[*He exits.*]

TERRY [*to* NORA, *a little panicked*]: Is he a threat? Tell me he's not a threat.

NORA: Everything's lost on you, isn't it?

[*Pause. They don't go into it.*]

TERRY: Well this has turned out to be one hell of a New Year's. I tell you what—he's never setting foot in this house again.

[*He picks up the cigars.*]

He took half of them.

[*He goes into his study.* NORA *looks at the mess* PETE *made.*]

NORA: I think he broke this.

[*She starts picking up the candles. If* TERRY *can be seen through his study door, he does the following. Otherwise, he can be heard.*]

TERRY [*off*]: It's after New Year's right? I can work now?

[*Beat.*]

[*Looking at his computer*] I didn't put this on "sleep."

NORA [*absently*]: What?

TERRY [*off*]: I asked you to keep the kids off of this.

[TERRY *types a password to open his email.*]

It's not a toy.

[*The computer gives a beep to indicate that* TERRY *has new mail. He studies the screen. Beat.*]

What the fuck does he want?

[NORA *realizes what* TERRY's *looking at. She stands up straight.*]

NORA: No. Oh God . . .

[*She starts for the study but stops, looks around, desperate. Then she grabs her coat and starts to run toward the back door.*]

TERRY [*off*]: Nora!

[*She stops. He enters and stares at her.*]

What have you done?

[*She starts to run, but he catches her, holds her.*]

NORA: Let me go—I'll go to the lake—I'll swim out in the lake—

TERRY: Tell me what you've done!

NORA: You can blame me—say you didn't know—

TERRY: Goddamn it! Stand still and tell me what you did!

[NORA *stops.*]

NORA: I've loved you more than anything else in the world.

TERRY: Don't give me that crap.

NORA: I borrowed money—

TERRY: From a client!

NORA: To save you!

TERRY: From Raj! Do you know what this means?

NORA: Yes.

TERRY: It means I'm his. From now on—whatever he wants! What were you thinking?

NORA [*steadily*]: You were sick—

TERRY [*overlapping*]: You stupid bitch. You weren't thinking. You never think!

NORA [*quietly*]: You didn't remember things I told you. You dropped Skyler.

TERRY: This is something your father would pull. This has his slimy little fingerprints all over it. He never left you a dime, did he?

NORA: I'll go to the lake.

TERRY: And drown yourself? Fuck that. What good would that do? I'm implicated up to my eyeballs. I'm out on my ass, which means no salary, no bonus, no assets. I have no assets!

[*He picks up* NORA's *wig.*]

Just debt debt debt!

[*He starts to hit her with the wig.*]

And you're the biggest liability of them all! A hundred thousand dollars? For what?

NORA: Your rehab.

TERRY: Where'd the rest of it go?

NORA: The condo.

TERRY: Ten percent down—where's—that's still not seventy grand. You're ten grand short.

NORA: The extras.

TERRY: Oh my God! You couldn't live without the granite so you ruin me?!

NORA: You wanted it too.

TERRY: So for the rest of my life I'll have to pay for you? So I don't go to prison over a . . . a Jacuzzi tub? I have to pay for you to Raj Patel? I'm forever in thrall to a couple of retards!

[*The phone rings.*]

What now?

[*He looks at the caller ID.*]

It's him.

[*He answers the phone.*]

You win, okay? You and my cunt of a wife—you beat me, okay? Tell me what you want—

[RAJ *stops* TERRY. TERRY *listens.*]

Don't fuck with me, Raj. I swear to God, if you fuck with me—

[RAJ *stops him again. Beat.*]

Why would you do that?

[*Long pause.*]

[*Quietly*] That is lucky. It is.

[*Small beat.*]

I want the note. The original and copies . . . Okay . . . Okay. Tomorrow morning. Listen—

[RAJ *stops him.*]

But I want to thank you . . . Okay.

[TERRY *hangs up the phone.*]

NORA: What is it?

TERRY [*to himself*]: He's not going to . . . he's not going to do anything. He doesn't—he's dropping it. [*To* NORA] Do we trust him?

NORA: Kristine—

TERRY: Talked him out of it.

[TERRY *laughs.*]

They love each other.

[*He breathes.*]

See? I told you she was smart.

NORA: You said she was boring.

TERRY: Oh my God! I'm saved! I'm totally saved! Oh man! Oh . . .

[*He picks up the phone quickly.*]

Does he still want the balance? How much do you owe him?

NORA: I don't know.

[TERRY, *not listening, hangs up the phone.*]

TERRY: No, he said he's dropping it.

[*He looks at her.*]

You don't know?

NORA: I've paid it off in dribs and drabs.

TERRY: You don't even—

[*He stops himself.*]

Ah forget it. The point is I'm saved.

[*He flops down on the couch, exhausted.*]

I feel like I'm going to have a heart attack. I seriously do.

[*He takes a deep breath.*]

Hey, I'm sorry I said all that stuff. I was really mad. I shouldn't have said that. And I forgive you, okay? I totally forgive you. I'm sure you didn't know, you know. And I'm sure he lied to you.

NORA: He didn't lie to me.

TERRY: But you didn't understand—

NORA: I understood.

TERRY: Then I said it, you know, I wasn't there to take care of you. And that's where I fell down. So that's what I'm saying. I forgive you.

NORA: Thanks.

[NORA *heads off.*]

TERRY: Where're you going?

NORA: To change.

[*She exits through the hall door. He talks at her from the living room.*]

TERRY: Good, let's, let's try to get back to normal here.

[*He goes to the kitchen.*]

I need a beer.

[*He opens the refrigerator.*]

See? I like this refrigerator. I don't know why people are so geeked up about Sub-Zero. [*Getting his beer, walking back into the living room*] I like everything about our place. I mean, I didn't want to live in Albany Park either. Who does? I was happy when I thought we had your dad's money. Not happy he was dead, of course. I kind of enjoyed him, actually. The guy was larger than life or whatever, which—some of that is cute. But too much of it and—Jesus fucking Christ—you just about kill me with it, you know? I mean, I'm not saying—I mean, calm down and focus and you can do whatever you set your mind to. Essentially—I've always known you were really capable. Like, sure, you could be a decorator or whatever it is you want to do, with the stuff . . . I don't know. Like here—you've done a great job with everything here. The fruit of my labor, as it were.

[*He sits on the couch again.*]

I like this couch. I like this table.

[*He laughs.*]

I swear. I feel like I've lost my mind and found it again, you know?

[NORA *enters in jeans, shoes in hand.*]

Why are you wearing that?

NORA [*sitting down to put on her shoes*]: I'm going.

TERRY: Out?

NORA: Over to Kristine's. I'll spend the night there. Then tomorrow I'll come back and pack.

TERRY: Pack?

NORA: Pete was right. You treat me like crap.

TERRY: You're running off with Pete?

NORA: No, I'm running off by myself. I'm leaving.

TERRY: You're leaving me?

NORA: Are you deaf?

TERRY: No. I'm just . . . [*Laughing*] You're leaving me?

NORA: Why is that funny?

TERRY: Because I yelled at you? I always yell at you. That doesn't mean anything.

NORA: You called me a cunt.

TERRY: I was justifiably angry—

NORA: You called me a retarded cunt.

TERRY: In the heat of the moment . . .

[*Beat.*]

What? I'm supposed to forget that you almost destroyed our lives?

NORA: Or maybe you could remember that I saved yours.

TERRY: Don't act so noble. There was something in it for you too.

NORA: Yeah. Not having a husband who was freaked out on drugs.

TERRY: I wasn't "freaked out"—

NORA: A husband who twists his knee playing basketball and that's all it takes to turn him into a drug addict. "Oh look, No-No. Is it swollen? I think it's swollen."

TERRY: It hurt like hell.

NORA: No-No. Your nickname for me is a scold.

TERRY: I thought you liked it.

NORA: A scold for a wayward child. It's something my father would say.

TERRY: Mommy. Little boy. You like stuff like that.

NORA [*realizing something, almost as if she has to shake it off*]: I'm a child. That's what I am.

[*She looks around.*]

This is my . . . this is my playhouse, my dollhouse. And I'm your little doll—I'm your doll and you can pick me up and play with me—pull my legs apart and slap me on the ass—and then when you're through with me throw me in the corner. I'm like a dog, who comes to you saying, "Pet me, pet me"—

TERRY: Are you a doll or a dog?

NORA: I'm a fucking personal assistant. Is what I am. A gofer! I pick up the dry cleaning, I make sure the refrigerator's stocked—I wait around for the cable guy and the alarm guy and have heart-to-heart discussions with the Perma-Seal guy and then, I get in the car and drive all over town to make sure these *toddlers* keep their *appointments*—!

TERRY: Oh yeah, life's hard, isn't it, No-No? Every day you have to get up and—oh! go to spin class, and oh!—get a Starbucks. How do you even have the energy for your pedicure?

NORA: You have no idea what I do with my days.

TERRY: And you have no idea what I do with mine! You're my doll? Well I'm your pack mule. You feel kept? I feel used! The shit I eat, every day, so you can go shopping—

NORA: The energy I use to stay cheerful. And to lie! Lie lie lie—it's all I ever do.

TERRY: Finally! She tells the truth!

NORA: Not that lie. Lies you make me tell. That you're stronger than me and smarter than me. That I need you more than you need me.

[*She looks at him.*]

And big lies. Real lies. That this is what I wanted. That I'm happy with this.

TERRY: You've never been happy?

NORA: I've been married.

TERRY: Well, if this isn't what you wanted, then tell me, please, what do you want? Because nobody put a gun to your head. If you're not happy—

NORA [*sarcastically*]: Being a wife and a mother—

TERRY: Then what else do you want?

NORA: To be a human being!

TERRY: It's the twenty-first century, Nora. Go ahead!

[*Long pause.*]

So where will you go?

NORA: What?

TERRY: You're leaving me. Where are you going?

NORA: I don't know yet.

TERRY: The condo's in my name. I'm sitting tight.

NORA: I can't wait to move.

TERRY: You're taking the kids, aren't you?

NORA: Of course.

TERRY: You'll get child support, but . . . you're leaving me. I don't see any alimony.

NORA: I'll get a job.

TERRY: Doing what?

NORA: I'll find something.

TERRY: Sure. I mean, it's not like you haven't worked in six years. Your computer skills are crack. Your Excel. Your PowerPoint. Your QuickBooks Pro.

NORA: I'll go back to the gallery.

TERRY: I remember that job at the gallery. Twenty grand a year. Before taxes. That would cover, let's see . . . well, it wouldn't cover Marta's salary so what are you going to do with the kids during the day? Leave the TV on and a bowl of cereal on the floor?

NORA: Have you ever heard of day care?

TERRY: You'd do that? That surprises me, because you told me part of the reason you've always felt unloved and unwanted was because you lost your mom when you were so little and so the last thing you wanted to do was leave your children alone—

NORA: Then I'll be poor. Okay? If that's the trade-off then I'll be poor. I don't need any of this. You know what all this is? It's a reproach. It's disgusting. I paid for every bit of it with my self-respect.

TERRY: Wow. You are woman, hear you roar. I'm going to get you one of those T-shirts that says, THIS IS WHAT A FEMINIST LOOKS LIKE.

NORA: Why have I been so afraid of you?

TERRY: Go out and tear up the world, Nora. Tear it up on six dollars an hour and public schools and plastic shoes from Payless. You'll have your self-respect then.

NORA: I hate you.

[Beat.]

TERRY: Yeah. Well. It's mutual.

NORA: You are losing your hair.

[She picks up her purse.]

TERRY: I'm going to have to ask you for your credit cards. You are no longer an authorized user.

NORA: Everything's about money with you.

[NORA *takes out her wallet and hands over the cards. She stops and looks at her wallet.*]

TERRY: What's the matter? You need cab fare?

[*Beat. She stares at the empty wallet.*]

NORA: I'm taking the bus.

[*She turns on her heel.*]

TERRY: You don't even know where the bus stop is. You need exact change.

[NORA *puts on her coat.*]

It's going to be full of drunks and smelly guys. Throwing up. Leaning on you.

[NORA *exits through the entryway.* TERRY *follows, staying in view.*]

You're gonna have to wait forever. It's freezing outside. It's, like, owl service. One an hour—

[*The front door opens. A cold blast of air hits* TERRY. *He steps back.*]

Nora. Stop being insane.

[*A car alarm is going off in the distance.*]

You can stop now. Come back inside. [*Suddenly desperate*] Goddamn it! Don't go! I'll do anything you want, okay? Don't go! Nora!

[*The door slams. Long pause.* NORA *slowly reenters.*]

NORA: Thank me. For saving your life.

[*Beat.*]

Say, "Thank you, Nora, for saving my life."

TERRY [*hating it*]: Thank you for saving my life.

[*Pause.*]

Is that it?

NORA [*uncertainly*]: I'd like a drink.

TERRY: Okay.

[*Beat.*]

Okay. I'll get us both a drink.

[TERRY *moves to the liquor cabinet.*]

Scotch, or . . . maybe—do you want champagne?

NORA: I don't care.

TERRY: Do you want to take off your coat, or . . . ?

[NORA *hesitates, then takes off her coat. Relieved,* TERRY *goes to the refrigerator and gets champagne.*]

Okay. We'll make a toast. To new beginnings. You made your point. I made mine. We just let it go too far, is all. Said some things . . . we probably shouldn't have said . . .

[TERRY *lets out a tight laugh.*]

Right?

[*They're both quiet as he gets glasses, opens the champagne. He pours two glasses, hands one to* NORA.]

TERRY: To new beginnings.

[*They drink. Long pause.*]

What do you want to do tomorrow?

NORA: The kids want to go ice skating.

TERRY: I can take them. If you'd rather do something else.

NORA: I can't.

TERRY: What?

NORA: I don't have any money.

TERRY: How much—

NORA: I need you to give me some money.

[*Pause. Then* TERRY *gets the credit cards he took from her. He hands them back to her.* NORA *takes them. Then she picks up her champagne glass, finishes it off, and pours herself another.* TERRY *still has a full glass.* NORA *holds out the bottle.*]

Drink up.

TERRY: What?

NORA: It doesn't keep.

TERRY: Right.

[TERRY *drinks his champagne.* NORA *refills his glass. They stand, holding their champagne.*]

NORA: You're going to pay for this.

TERRY: I know.

[*They don't look at each other. The lights slowly fade.*]

Nora (Maggie Siff) shows off her new purchases to Terry (Anthony Starke).

Raj (Firdous Bamji) threatens to reveal Nora's secret.

Nora does her *Flashdance* routine for Dr. Pete (Lance Stuart Baker, filming) and Terry.

Terry turns on Nora after he discovers she's been lying to him.